EVERY TIME twenty-year-old Eitan Bernath tastes something, he immediately thinks, *How can I make this myself?* From burgers to beer bread, tacos to mushroom cheesesteaks, and every kind of potato preparation you can imagine, Eitan has obsessively created and re-created all the amazing flavors and textures he loves, and shares them with infectious energy and insatiable curiosity for his millions of fans across social media.

In Eitan's debut cookbook, he channels his passion for all things delicious into inventive and approachable comfort food recipes that range from new twists on classics to his version of dishes from around the world that he has meticulously studied with friends, neighbors, and other chefs.

Overflowing with positivity, creativity, and the "You can definitely do this!" attitude that catapulted Eitan into the media spotlight, *Eitan Eats the World* will charm and inspire readers to get in the kitchen and start having fun.

"Eitan's cooking style has set the bar for delicious home-cooked food. I love his pace and energy and I believe he inspires a whole new generation to approach food with curiosity and passion. His skill set and joy make a perfect combination!"

—DREW BARRYMORE, actor, TV host, and author

"Eitan's passion for cooking is so irresistible; it's impossible not to get excited about food with this book! The recipes in *Eitan Eats the World* strike such a delicious balance of creativity and comfort, and all of them are totally crave-able. Also, there's tahini puppy chow! YES, *PLEASE!!!*"

—MOLLY YEH, cookbook author and Food Network host

Eitan Eats the World

EitanEats
the World

EITAN BERNATH

PHOTOGRAPHS BY MARK WEINBERG

Clarkson Potter/Publishers
New York

Dedicated in loving memory of Grandpa Larry:
Your enduring support, encouragement, and love
made this book possible. Everyone who met you left
with a smile on their face, and I hope that this book
brings its readers even a fraction of that joy.

Contents

Introduction

I was wildly fortunate to grow up with parents who pursued their own passions, and so my early love for food and cooking was nurtured and supported from a very young age. With a mom who's a high-school math teacher and a dad who's a pediatric occupational therapist, it was natural for my parents to turn every activity into an opportunity for education and research. On any given Sunday afternoon, you'd find the four of us piled in the car on our way to a vegetarian Indian restaurant, for my family's favorite cuisine. We traveled all around the tri-state area to try restaurants with different regional specialties, and my parents wisely encouraged me and my brother to order new dishes each time as a way to learn about this large and diverse country from the most delicious kind of teacher: its food.

One Sunday we drove to a new restaurant that specialized in south Indian cuisine. Upon seeing the menu, I immediately noticed the food was different from what I was used to at the mostly north Indian restaurants we had visited before. "Where is all the bread? No naan? Roti? Poori?" I sputtered to my mom. But my initial confusion and, no joke, dismay turned around as soon as the food came to the table. In place of the bread were mountains of fragrant rice, lentils, and legume-heavy dishes. My taste buds were happy, and my curiosity about exactly *why* I was being served such different things was ignited. On the ride home that night, my mom, ever the teacher, explained to me that the difference in geography and climate across each part of a country as big as India results in a diversity of agriculture, and thus in cooking methods and cuisines. In the north of India, wheat grows in abundance, and in the south, lentils, rice, and other legumes flourish. So people in these two areas rely on different raw ingredients and consequently have different dishes as part of their regional cuisines.

In the days and weeks after that meal, I did what any other eight-year-old would do: I spent hours watching documentary after documentary about the differences between the cuisines of the north and the south. You know, a typical Sunday night activity for a third grader. The more I discovered about the intersection of food, culture, and geography, the more fascinated I became with knowing about *other* places and the culinary traditions of each of them. Through learning about food, I was expanding my understanding of the world, traveling thousands of miles and circling the globe to try all sorts of amazing new things. (Or at least it felt like that!) I constantly asked my mom to make dishes I saw on TV or tried during our Sunday outings. She did cook them, but she also encouraged me to try to make them myself—and this was when I had the lightbulb moment that, as much as I loved eating and learning about food, actually cooking it myself was the ultimate level of fun.

As my family will attest, I take everything to the nth degree. Curiosity, thoroughness, and—I'll admit—a tendency to turn interests into obsessions are my defining characteristics. So for the rest of my childhood, instead of being on the basketball court or in front of a video game console, I could often be found in my room, feverishly taking notes on a documentary about a small fishing village in the state of Goa on India's western coast. There were no baseball cards under my bed, but rather tawas, tortilla presses, and Indian spice boxes, and any authentic piece of cookware I could get my hands on. All my holiday and birthday gifts while growing up were tools to cook with or resources to teach me about cooking. The kitchen became my favorite place to be.

Okay, so I do have another defining characteristic: When I get obsessed with something, I am *super* excited about it—and I don't want to keep that excitement to myself. So I didn't want all the fascinating things I was learning and cooking to be limited to my kitchen. I wanted to be like the chefs I saw on TV: to share the passion and enthusiasm I have for ALL food with as many people as possible. Luckily, I didn't have to wait that long: I made my debut TV appearance at eleven years old on the first-ever kids' episode of *Chopped.* In a matter of days, little Eitan went from cooking in his parents' home kitchen to cooking on the Food Network. And while I may have lost on *Chopped*, it was the biggest win of my life, because it was the spark that lit the flame of my culinary ambitions: to develop my own platform to connect with people about food.

At first, social media was the answer. I began documenting my culinary journeys first on a blog, then on Instagram and Facebook. I posted articles and pictures of what I was cooking and couldn't believe how many people responded to them. I knew my family and friends enjoyed seeing me cook, but strangers, too? One hundred followers turned into one thousand. A thousand turned into five thousand. Five thousand turned into ten thousand. Ten thousand turned into one hundred thousand. It didn't stop. I realized that as much as I wanted to connect with lots of people through my cooking, lots of people *also* wanted to watch me cook. I had started a race with my passion that had no finish line. So I kept racing.

From my experiences on the Food Network, I knew how much I loved being on camera, so I decided to make the leap to YouTube and recorded my first cooking video. Before I posted it, I got nervous about people's reactions, especially the kids at my school. Did I look stupid on camera? What were people going to think of me? Would anyone even watch it? But I didn't let my insecurities get in the way of doing something I loved—a lesson that has stuck with me ever since. The response to that video was overwhelmingly positive, and the engagement on the post was my highest ever. Knowing that I'd been able to bring my passion into so many other people's lives, and that I was getting them as excited about cooking as I was, motivated me to keep striving for new audiences online, on TV, in media—and it's why I was so excited to have the opportunity to write this book.

One thing that's remained consistent since my first attempts in the kitchen as an eight-year-old is my penchant for comfort food. Comfort foods were what I gravitated toward in my early cooking days, because they are both delicious and approachable for an aspiring chef. I define comfort food as food that warms the heart, satisfies the stomach, and feeds the soul. And I'm lucky to have grown up in a family who not only encouraged my passion for learning about the cuisines of places geographically far away but who also had their own dishes and food traditions that I treasure—and which became my first comfort foods as well.

Yet while comfort food in some form or other has universal appeal, part of my education in cooking has been learning that what constitutes comfort food differs wildly not only by the country but even more so by the cultures and distinct region of its origin. Comfort foods—which can be anything from your favorite childhood meal to the dish you crave after a long, hard day—are an essential part of learning about cuisines from around the world, beyond the Americanized menu versions of dishes that are often eaten at restaurants. I wanted to learn what other families make for a weeknight dinner, the favorite snack that the people of a country or a continent away grab when they're out and about running errands, or a hot one-bowl meal that might have some unfamiliar ingredients but speaks the international language of comfort. I would never pretend to be an expert in every cuisine, so this cookbook is truly a tribute to all the foods I currently love the most. All the recipes in this book, no matter their origins, were developed out of my previously mentioned curiosity with figuring out how dishes work. As you'll see all over this book, most of these recipes had their beginnings when I tasted a new dish or was introduced to a new technique, and then I meticulously (some might say *obsessively*) figured out how to replicate it as authentically as possible at home. These recipes are also a testament to my never-ending desire to learn about not only the food but the people who turn to these dishes when they crave a little comfort.

One other thing that comes up in this book is how I used to be a *very* picky eater. Yes, that is correct: your boy who now cooks with spice, heat, and vegetables used to basically live on cereal, bread, and potatoes. So part of my own journey as a cook has been the massive expansion of my palate and being open to trying new foods and flavors. One of the reasons I wanted to write this book was to inspire other little Eitans who might be picky or intimidated by cooking to get in the kitchen and try new things! This cookbook is truly a collection of the foods that I crave, the recipes I turn to for comfort, the dishes that excite me, and the type of meal I'd make if I could invite each and every one of you over for dinner. I hope these recipes become the ones that you also turn to for comfort and that you share with friends and family, and most importantly—I hope they help you discover the FUN of preparing a delicious meal.

Eitan Bernath

Eitan Essentials

Before we get to the good stuff—the food!—I want to take a few minutes to share lessons I've learned, especially during the course of making this book. I am mostly self-taught, and I've learned *a lot* through trial and error (you may have seen me make a mess or two in my videos), so I'm sharing tips, tools, and hacks that will help you avoid some of the mistakes I've made through the learning process. If you want a happier, tidier, and overall more successful cooking experience, here are my twelve kitchen essentials.

1. **READ THE RECIPE!** As someone who gets easily excited about cooking, I know it can be tempting to immediately jump into a recipe before first reading it through to the end. Resist that temptation! I promise it's worth the extra five minutes to make sure you know where the recipe is going to take you.

2. **TASTE YOUR FOOD.** Tasting as you cook is super important in ensuring you are happy with the final taste of the dish. Little tasting spoons are great in the kitchen; they enable you to quickly and easily determine how the seasonings should be adjusted.

3. **DON'T SKIMP ON SALT (OR PEPPER).** Speaking of seasonings, not all salt is created equal! If you are still cooking with iodized table salt, it's time for you to upgrade to some good old kosher salt! Not only is it what most recipes mean when they call for salt, but its flavor and texture result in much better seasoned food. Plus, while you're at it, swap out the preground pepper for a pepper mill and grind it yourself for improved freshness and flavor every time!

4. **CLEAN AS YOU COOK.** This may sound like something a parent would nag you about, but it makes the entire cooking process—before, during, and after—*so* much easier. Any time I've made a mistake or accidentally spilled something while cooking, it's usually because I wasn't cleaning as I cooked!

5. **SHARPER KNIFE = SAFER KNIFE.** Having sharp knives is one of the keys to being safe while cooking. Believe it or not, a dull knife is more dangerous than a sharp one! Dull knives can slip easily because they have a harder time cutting into the food. This loss in precision can very quickly result in a cut.

6. STABILIZE YOUR CUTTING BOARD! Using a sharp chef's knife can be intimidating, and a cutting board that slides all over your counter while you're trying to mince onions makes it even harder. I like to place a damp paper towel underneath mine to stabilize it while cooking. A rubber drawer liner is also a great, reusable option!

7. BUY AN INSTANT-READ THERMOMETER. This super-inexpensive tool takes the guesswork out of baking, cooking meat, chocolate work, and even sugar work in a pinch.

8. INVEST IN CAST-IRON COOKWARE. The quality of your equipment in the kitchen is just as important as the quality of your ingredients. Enameled cast-iron pots and pans are extremely versatile and ensure even and consistent temperatures while cooking. There is almost nothing you can't use them for in the kitchen!

9. MICROPLANES ARE GRATE. Most people see these and think citrus zester, but a Microplane is a great tool for a finely grated shower of cheese and—my personal favorite—grating garlic or fresh ginger. It's faster AND easier than mincing them with a knife!

10. RULERS RULE. As the son of a math teacher, we always had a lot of rulers around the house, and it turns out they're also super useful in the kitchen! If you don't have one already, it's a tiny investment, and it comes in handy in so many recipes, including cutting the pie dough for my Blueberry Cardamom Hand Pies (page 219) and measuring the pizza dough in my Pizza with Spicy Italian Crumble (page 166).

11. SMALL-BATCH YOUR SPICES. You may notice there are a lot of spices in this book. When I was younger, I got very excited about spices and used to purchase them in bulk, but in fact, it's best to buy spices in small quantities. Spices very quickly go bad and lose a lot of their intensity, so the smaller your container, the more often you're replacing, which ensures freshness and flavor.

12. EXPAND YOUR WHISK HORIZONS. I love a multipurpose kitchen tool, and a whisk can do a lot more than beat eggs. I use mine for everything from mashing avocados for guacamole to smashing the clumps out of lumpy brown sugar.

BREAK

First, let me be clear about something: I have great respect and appreciation for a simple breakfast! I will never be above a humble bowl of cereal. However, breakfast can also be *way* more exciting and elaborate when the occasion or mood calls for it. And don't worry: the recipes in this chapter are built around all our favorite breakfast staples—eggs, bread, fruit, plenty of potatoes, and, of course, cereal—so you still get the comforting familiarity we all need in the morning, but in tastier, reimagined ways.

If you want to impress friends for brunch, the **Green Shakshuka** (page 26) is the way to go! If you're up for a little science experiment, the **English Muffins with Homemade Butter & Strawberry Jam** (page 30) will teach you how to make all three from SCRATCH, and if you want something easy but more interesting than a granola bar, the **Coconut Yogurt Breakfast Ice Pops** (page 42) are basically a ready-made smoothie bowl on a stick. If you're dead set on cereal for breakfast, might I recommend you try the **Cornflake-Crusted French Toast** (page 33)? As someone who's woken up ready to eat every single day of his life, I've got a breakfast recipe for every kind of craving and every kind of morning.

FAST ALL DAY

Heavenly Cinnamon Rolls

● **MAKES 12 ROLLS**

Let the record show, cinnamon rolls are my favorite baked good. Wait! No . . . cookies are! Wait! Cinnamon rolls. You know what? I love them equally, so I could never pick a favorite. There's room in my heart for both!

Now that that's settled, let's talk about this recipe. Cinnamon rolls are basically a comfort-food dessert you can sneak into breakfast: warm dough, gooey cinnamon filling, and tangy cream cheese icing. Now, for a perfect cinnamon roll, you have to start with a rich dough, and for that, you need rich ingredients. This dough is packed with butter and milk, and the double rise gives the dough a complex flavor and a tender but pillowy texture. Next, you have to find the perfect cinnamon to sugar ratio: too much sugar and you overpower the cinnamon, but too much cinnamon, and you have a roll that just tastes like spice. Finally, the cream cheese icing is a classic for a reason: It's the perfect touch to finish off the rolls with a bit more sweetness and some welcomed tang.

ROLLS

1 cup (244g) whole milk

1 (0.25-ounce) package active dry yeast

8 tablespoons (100g) granulated sugar

1½ teaspoons kosher salt

2 large eggs

2 sticks (220g) unsalted butter, at room temperature, plus more for greasing

4¾ cups (665g) all-purpose flour, plus more as needed

1½ cups (360g) firmly packed dark brown sugar

2 tablespoons ground cinnamon

ICING

4 ounces (113g) cream cheese, at room temperature

½ stick (55g) unsalted butter, at room temperature

½ teaspoon pure vanilla extract

¼ teaspoon kosher salt

2 cups (240g) confectioners' sugar

ASSEMBLY

1 large egg, beaten

1/ MAKE THE ROLLS In a small saucepan set over low heat, heat the milk until it is warm to the touch. (If you have a thermometer, it should be about 105°F, but no warmer than 110°F.) Pour the warmed milk into the bowl of a stand mixer and sprinkle the yeast and 1 tablespoon of the granulated sugar on top. Let it sit until foamy, about 5 minutes. Add the remaining 7 tablespoons sugar, the salt, eggs, 1 stick of the butter, and the flour and mix the ingredients on medium speed until they start to pull away from the sides of the bowl, adding more flour, 1 tablespoon at a time, as needed until the dough comes together, 2 to 3 minutes. Transfer the dough to a lightly floured surface and knead by hand until very smooth, 5 to 7 minutes.

2/ Grease a large bowl with butter and add the dough, turning to coat it all over. Cover with plastic wrap and set aside to rise in a warm place until doubled in size, about 1 hour.

3/ Grease a 9 × 13-inch glass or ceramic baking pan.

4/ Once risen, punch the dough down, then on a lightly floured surface, roll it out into a 24 × 12-inch rectangle.

5/ In a small bowl, combine the brown sugar and cinnamon. Spread the remaining stick of butter across the surface of the dough, spread into an even layer, and

recipe continues

top with the brown sugar–cinnamon mixture, pressing it down so it adheres to the dough.

6/ Tightly roll the dough up lengthwise, then cut it into 12 equal sections using a serrated knife. Nestle the cinnamon rolls cut-side up in the baking pan. Cover and let rise again in a warm place for 30 minutes. Preheat the oven to 350°F and place a rack in the center.

7/ MAKE THE ICING While the rolls are rising, in the bowl of a stand mixer fitted with the paddle attachment, beat the cream cheese and butter on medium speed until smooth and creamy, about 3 minutes. Add the vanilla and salt and mix on low to combine. Add the confectioners' sugar and mix on low until thoroughly combined, light, and fluffy, about 2 minutes.

8/ Brush the tops of the cinnamon rolls with the beaten egg. Bake until golden brown, about 30 minutes, rotating the pan front to back halfway through.

9/ Let the rolls cool for 5 minutes, then spread half of the icing over the rolls with an offset spatula or the back of a spoon. Let cool for another 15 to 20 minutes, then spread the remaining icing over the top and serve. (Leftover rolls can be stored in an airtight container at room temperature for up to 3 days.)

Green Shakshuka

First things first, let's address the most important question: *Eitan . . . why is it green?* For a few extremely delicious reasons! Trust me when I tell you this is the only time you'll want to eat green eggs. (We'll hold on the ham.) Traditionally, shakshuka—a dish of eggs baked in a spiced sauce, popular in North Africa and the Middle East—is made with a tomato base, but here I'm swapping the tomatoes for a blend of greens and fresh herbs. The resulting dish is everything you'd want for breakfast or brunch: zingy sauce, perfectly poached eggs, tangy feta, nutritious greens, and a tower of pita for dipping. Did I mention it's beautiful, too? Not only is it perfectly Instagrammable, it's definitely sharable.

Kosher salt

4 ounces fresh spinach
(about 4 cups packed)

1 large bunch Swiss chard, ribs and
stems discarded, leaves chopped
(about 6 cups)

2 tablespoons olive oil

1 medium yellow onion, thinly sliced
(about 2 cups)

3 large garlic cloves, thinly sliced

½ serrano pepper, diced (and
seeded, if less heat is desired)

1 teaspoon ground cumin

1 teaspoon caraway seeds

½ teaspoon crushed red pepper
flakes, plus more for serving, or
1 teaspoon harissa powder

Freshly ground black pepper

½ cup chopped fresh cilantro

½ cup chopped fresh flat-leaf parsley

½ cup heavy cream

Juice of ½ lemon

4 to 6 large eggs (see Quick Bite)

2 tablespoons crumbled feta cheese

Pita or crusty bread, for serving

1/ Bring a large pot of heavily salted water to a boil and fill a large bowl with ice water. Add the spinach and Swiss chard to the boiling water and blanch until the vegetables turn bright green, about 2 minutes. Use a long slotted spoon to transfer the greens to the ice water and, once cooled, drain them and squeeze out the excess moisture. Transfer the greens to a high-speed blender or food processor. Blend until completely puréed, about 30 seconds. Set aside.

2/ Heat the olive oil in a 10- to 12-inch nonstick or cast-iron skillet over medium heat. Add the onion and sauté until soft and translucent, about 7 minutes. Add the garlic and serrano pepper and sauté until fragrant, about 2 minutes. Add the cumin, caraway seeds, and red pepper flakes and cook until fragrant, about 1 minute. Season to taste with salt and black pepper.

3/ Add the puréed greens, cilantro, parsley, and 1 cup water to the skillet. Simmer until the mixture has reduced by half, 3 to 5 minutes.

4/ Stir in the heavy cream and cook until simmering, 2 minutes. Stir in the lemon juice, taste, and adjust salt and pepper.

5/ Using the back of a spoon, make a well in the pan for each egg, spacing the wells evenly apart. Reduce the heat to medium-low and gently crack one egg into each well and cook uncovered for 7 to 9 minutes, depending on the desired doneness of the eggs.

6/ Top with the crumbled feta and red pepper flakes. Serve immediately with pita.

QUICK BITE

This recipe is super flexible, so you can play around with the number of eggs, depending on what you're going for. If you're serving a big brunch, 6 eggs feed more friends; if you've got a smaller group (or if you're a little obsessed with the sauce like I am!), 4 eggs will hit the spot.

PB&J Pancakes

Before I start telling you about this recipe, I have a confession to make: I don't like peanut butter and jelly sandwiches. So, to redeem myself to the many of you who I'm sure are shocked and disappointed by this news, here's my recipe that combines those flavors in a way I *do* find delicious.

The peanut butter is blended into the pancake batter itself, which gives the pancake that familiar peanutty-ness and lends a moist, cakey texture to it. Instead of syrup, I combine jam with fresh raspberries for a sweet topping. Last thing: The buttermilk is essential for getting that rich, buttery flavor and perfect, deeply golden exterior. If you have a hard time finding it, check out the Quick Bite for a substitute.

RASPBERRY JAM

6 ounces (170g) fresh raspberries, plus more for serving

¼ cup (75g) grape jam

1 tablespoon pure maple syrup

1 tablespoon all-purpose flour

PANCAKES

1 cup (140g) all-purpose flour

2 teaspoons baking powder

1 teaspoon kosher salt

½ teaspoon baking soda

⅔ cup (170g) creamy peanut butter

1¼ cups (306g) full-fat buttermilk (see Quick Bite)

1 large egg

2 tablespoons pure maple syrup

2 tablespoons unsalted butter, melted

1 teaspoon pure vanilla extract

Nonstick cooking spray or coconut oil spray

Chopped salted peanuts, for serving

1/ MAKE THE JAM In a small saucepan, heat the raspberries, jam, and maple syrup over medium-low heat. In a small bowl, whisk the flour with 2 tablespoons water until the flour is dissolved. Whisk the flour mixture into the raspberry mixture and cook, stirring occasionally, until the raspberries break down and the mixture is thickened, about 10 minutes. Remove from the heat and set aside.

2/ MAKE THE PANCAKES In a large bowl, whisk together the flour, baking powder, salt, and baking soda. In a small microwave-safe bowl, microwave the peanut butter in 30-second intervals, stirring after each, until a thin, pourable consistency is achieved. In a medium bowl, whisk together the buttermilk, egg, ⅓ cup of the melted peanut butter, the maple syrup, butter, and vanilla. Pour the wet ingredients into the dry ones and fold until just barely combined, being sure not to overmix.

3/ Preheat the oven to 200°F and place a sheet pan inside. Spray a large nonstick skillet or griddle with cooking spray, then set it over medium heat. Using a measuring cup, measure ¼ cup of batter, pour it into the skillet, and cook until the pancake top bubbles and the bottom is golden brown, about 3 minutes. (Cook as many pancakes as possible without crowding or touching.) Flip and cook until the other side is golden brown, another 2 minutes. Transfer to the sheet pan in the oven to keep warm while you make the rest of the pancakes.

4/ When all the pancakes have been cooked, remove them from the oven and top each with raspberry jam, the remaining melted peanut butter, fresh raspberries, and chopped peanuts. Serve immediately.

QUICK BITE

Full-fat buttermilk is an absolute game-changer in this recipe, but I know it can be hard to find, depending on where you live. Don't worry! You can substitute the buttermilk with equal parts plain yogurt or sour cream and milk.

English Muffins

WITH HOMEMADE BUTTER & STRAWBERRY JAM

● **MAKES 10 MUFFINS**

English muffins are my current breakfast obsession. They will always have a leg up on toast because of the nooks and crannies! The edges get extra toasty, all the butter melts down into the muffin, and then you're left with lots of room for jam on top. I love that each bite is a little bit different, both in texture and in butter-to-jam ratio.

Since I'm hooked, I knew I had to develop a homemade version. Let me tell you, developing this recipe was a labor of love, but I promise it's worth the effort. Don't skimp on the overnight rise; that's the key to big flavor and, even more importantly, the only way to get big bubbles in the dough that turn into those essential nooks and crannies. I know thinking about breakfast the day before might seem crazy, but that rise is essential to get the correct final texture. Finally, to get that iconic shape and golden exterior, the muffins are griddled on both sides before they finish baking in the oven.

1½ cups (365g) whole milk

1½ tablespoons sugar

1 (0.25-ounce) packet active dry yeast

½ stick (55g) unsalted butter, at room temperature, plus more for greasing

1 large egg

3¾ cups (525g) bread flour, plus more for kneading

2 teaspoons kosher salt

Nonstick cooking spray

Cornmeal, for dusting

SERVING

Strawberry Jam (recipe follows)

Homemade Butter (recipe follows)

1/ In a small saucepan, heat the milk over low heat until it is warm to the touch. (If you have a thermometer, it should be about 105°F, but no warmer than 110°F.) Pour the warmed milk into the bowl of a stand mixer and sprinkle with the sugar and yeast. Let sit until foamy, about 5 minutes. Add the butter, egg, flour, and salt. Using the dough hook, mix on medium speed until a rough dough forms, 3 to 5 minutes. Turn the dough out onto a lightly floured surface and knead for about 5 minutes, until smooth. The dough should still be slightly wet and sticky.

2/ Grease a large bowl with butter. Transfer the dough to the bowl. Grease a layer of plastic wrap with cooking spray and cover the dough, oiled side down. Let rise on the counter for 1 hour, or until doubled in size.

3/ Line two sheet pans with parchment paper and dust generously with cornmeal. Lightly oil your hands with cooking spray or a little bit of neutral oil, then turn out the risen dough onto a work surface sprayed with cooking spray. Cut the dough into 10 equal-size pieces. Fold the corners of a piece of dough into the middle to form a ball, then turn the ball over seam-side down and, using your hand, gently apply pressure and roll a few times to tighten the seams. (Each ball of dough should be about 3 inches across.) Place the ball on a sheet pan. Repeat with the remaining dough, spacing the pieces out evenly on both sheet pans. Sprinkle the tops with cornmeal, lightly cover them with plastic wrap, and refrigerate overnight.

4/ Remove the dough from the refrigerator and let sit for 30 minutes to come to room temperature.

5/ Preheat the oven to 350°F. Heat a large cast-iron skillet or griddle over low heat. Working in batches of 3 or 4 and, using a spatula, carefully transfer the pieces

recipe continues

of dough to the skillet, being careful not to deflate the dough or let the cornmeal fall off. Cook until the bottoms of the muffins are dark golden brown, 5 to 7 minutes. Flip and cook the other side until it is dark golden brown as well, 5 to 7 minutes more.

6/ Discard the parchment paper, then using a spatula place the browned muffins back onto the sheet pans and repeat with the remaining dough. Bake the English muffins until the sides look dry and the tops and bottoms are deeply golden brown, 5 to 10 minutes. Transfer them to a wire rack and let the muffins cool to room temperature. Split the muffins through the middle and serve with the jam and butter. (The muffins will keep in an airtight container or resealable plastic bag at room temperature for 3 days. They can also be wrapped individually in foil, placed in a resealable bag, and frozen.)

MAKES 2 CUPS

Strawberry Jam

Jam couldn't be easier to make from scratch. It's just three ingredients, and the pectin in the fruit acts as a natural thickening agent, so the result is a deep, fruity flavor. My favorite flavor is strawberry, but feel free to use your own preferred berry. Jam is also a great way to use up fruit in your refrigerator that's a day or two from going bad.

1 pound fresh strawberries, stemmed and quartered	**½ cup sugar** **Juice of ½ lemon**

1/ In a medium pot set over medium heat, combine the strawberries, sugar, and lemon juice. Bring to a boil, then reduce the heat to low and simmer for 5 to 7 minutes, until the strawberries are soft.

2/ Once the strawberries are soft, mash them slightly with a potato masher. Increase the heat to medium so the mixture comes to a light boil (not roiling), and cook for an additional 10 to 15 minutes, stirring almost continuously, until thickened. Pour the mixture into a heatproof, resealable jar, let cool, then refrigerate for a few hours until the jam thickens and sets. (The jam can be stored in an airtight container in the refrigerator for 2 to 3 weeks.)

MAKES ABOUT 1 CUP

Homemade Butter

Making your own butter is arguably over the top, but if you're going to make the other two from scratch, why not just go all the way? Homemade butter is like a science experiment: While beating, the heavy cream separates into butterfat and buttermilk, and suddenly you've got butter! Now you have an incredibly delicious, 100 percent homemade breakfast for the week!

1 quart heavy cream	**Pinch of salt (optional)**

1/ In the bowl of a stand mixer fitted with the whisk attachment, add the heavy cream. Beat the cream on medium speed, then once it begins to thicken, raise the speed to high and continue beating until the butterfat separates from the liquid, 5 to 10 minutes total. Remove the butterfat from the bowl. If using salt, discard the liquid from the bowl, rinse it with water, dry, then return the butterfat to the bowl and fold in a generous pinch of salt.

2/ Transfer the butter to a large piece of plastic wrap and form it into a log shape. Tightly roll the butter in the plastic wrap and place it in the refrigerator until you are ready to use it. (The butter can be stored in the refrigerator for up to 3 weeks.)

Cornflake-Crusted French Toast

As a kid, I was obsessed with cereal. Now that I'm older, I've upgraded my breakfast game so that when I have a cereal craving, this French toast is my favorite way to satisfy it. The cornflake coating on the challah creates an amazing crunch that stands up to almost any amount of syrup that drowns it. Challah is my favorite bread to use for French toast because of its soft, pillowy texture, which contrasts well with the crunchy cornflake coating. Note: You can swap another flaky cereal for cornflakes. Just make sure it's not too sugary, or the cereal coating will burn when you cook the French toast.

4 large eggs

1 cup (244g) whole milk

⅓ cup (65g) sugar

2 teaspoons ground cinnamon

2 teaspoons pure vanilla extract

1 teaspoon kosher salt

4 cups cornflakes

8 (1-inch-thick) slices challah bread

½ stick (55g) unsalted butter

Whipped cream, assorted berries, and pure maple syrup, for serving

1/ In a wide bowl, whisk together the eggs, milk, sugar, cinnamon, vanilla, and salt. Set aside. Add the cornflakes to another wide bowl and crush them slightly with your hands.

2/ Working with one slice of challah at a time, dip a piece into the egg mixture, submerge it for 30 seconds, then flip the bread and repeat so that both sides are completely coated. Remove the bread from the egg mixture and let the excess liquid drip off, then transfer it to the crushed cornflakes, coating it completely on both sides. Place the coated bread slice on a sheet pan and repeat with the remaining challah slices.

3/ Preheat the oven to 200°F and place a clean sheet pan inside. Heat a large nonstick frying pan over medium-low heat. Add 1 tablespoon of the butter and let it melt. Once melted, add two slices of challah to the pan and cook on each side for 2 to 3 minutes, until both sides are golden brown. Once cooked, transfer them to the sheet pan in the oven to keep warm and repeat with the remaining butter and slices. Once all the slices are cooked, serve immediately with whipped cream, berries, and maple syrup.

Perfect Soft Scrambled Eggs on Toast

● SERVES 2

For my first sixteen years on Earth, I only had scrambled eggs one way, and that was fully cooked. But after trying soft scrambled eggs for the first time, I immediately understood why people cook their eggs this way. Soft scrambling eggs—a method of cooking eggs at a lower temperature, stirring constantly—turns them into something else entirely: They're creamy and spreadable, almost custardy. They taste as if they're loaded with heavy cream or butter, but they aren't! Perfect for topping a big piece of toast for breakfast, they're an easy way to change up your go-to egg-cooking method. But what I love most about them is that they require constant attention for the few minutes they're cooking, so some days, it may be the only time I'm not looking at a screen or thinking about what's next on my to-do list. Soft scrambled eggs can be your morning meditation. You heard it here first!

4 large eggs

Kosher salt

2 tablespoons unsalted butter

2 (½-inch-thick) slices sourdough bread, toasted

SERVING

Flaky sea salt

Freshly ground black pepper

Crushed red pepper flakes

Thinly sliced chives

1/ Crack the eggs into a medium bowl and add 4 pinches of kosher salt (a pinch per egg). Using a whisk, whip the eggs until completely combined and pale yellow in color, 60 to 90 seconds.

2/ In a small nonstick frying pan set over medium-low heat, melt the butter. Once the butter is barely foaming, add the eggs and cook, stirring continuously with a heatproof rubber spatula, until small curds form and the eggs are moist and just barely set, about 2 minutes.

3/ Using a spoon, divide the eggs between pieces of toast, then top with flaky salt, black pepper, red pepper flakes, and chives. Serve immediately.

Beet Rostï

● SERVES 4

First things first, we need to acknowledge where this dish comes from—history lesson time! Rostï is a breakfast dish from Switzerland that is similar to a huge hash brown or latke. First eaten by Swiss farmers to fuel them for a long day's work, the original recipe includes just two ingredients: potatoes and a fat to fry them in (usually butter). And while those are arguably two of the best ingredients in the world, you know I had to put my own spin on it!

Beets sometimes get a bad rap, but trust me, this recipe will change your mind. They give the final product a beautiful color, so it's a great centerpiece for an impressive breakfast. They also add a delicate sweetness but are still earthy like the potatoes, so they make a perfect pairing. Think of this recipe as hash browns' fancy European aunt!

1 pound russet potatoes (about 3 medium), peeled

1 pound red beets (about 2 medium), trimmed and peeled

½ cup all-purpose flour

1½ teaspoons kosher salt

½ teaspoon freshly ground black pepper

2 tablespoons vegetable oil

2 tablespoons unsalted butter

½ cup crème fraîche

1 tablespoon chopped fresh dill

Zest and juice of 1 lemon

Flaky sea salt

1/ On the large holes of a box grater or in a food processor fitted with the grating attachment, grate the potatoes and transfer them to a large bowl. Cover with cold water and let sit for 10 minutes. While the potatoes soak, grate the beets on the same side of the box grater or through the food processor. Transfer them to a fine-mesh strainer and press them, squeezing with your hands or the back of a spoon to extract as much moisture as possible. Set them aside in a large bowl.

2/ Once the potatoes have soaked for 10 minutes, carefully pour off the water, taking care not to disrupt the starch that has collected at the bottom of the bowl. Working one handful at a time, press the potatoes in the fine-mesh strainer, extracting as much moisture as possible. Add the drained potatoes to the beets, then add the potato starch that has collected at the bottom of the bowl to the shredded potatoes and beets.

3/ Sprinkle the flour, salt, and pepper over the beets and potatoes and toss to thoroughly combine.

4/ Place a 12-inch nonstick or oil-coated cast-iron skillet over medium-high heat and add 1 tablespoon of the oil and 1 tablespoon of the butter. Once the butter melts, add the beets and potatoes, spreading them into an even layer that fills up the entire pan. Reduce the heat to medium and cook, undisturbed, until the vegetables are very crisp, 6 to 8 minutes, rotating the pan every so often to prevent burning. Once the potatoes have crisped on the first side, remove the pan from the heat. Working with caution, top the skillet with a large platter or rimless sheet pan and carefully flip the rostï out onto the platter.

5/ Return the pan to medium-high heat and add the remaining 1 tablespoon oil and 1 tablespoon butter. Once the butter melts, carefully slide the rostï back into the pan, uncooked-side down. Cook, undisturbed, until the underside is very crisp, 6 to 8 minutes more.

6/ Carefully slide the rostï out of the pan onto a serving dish. Top with the crème fraîche, fresh dill, and lemon zest and juice, then sprinkle with flaky salt. Serve warm.

Craggy Breakfast Potatoes

● SERVES 4 TO 6

Potatoes are my favorite vegetable (if you want to argue the merits of potatoes as a vegetable, my DMs are open), so whenever I'm making a savory breakfast, they're the first ingredient I think of—though let's be honest, I'll eat them any time of day!

What sets these potatoes apart is the craggy, crunchy texture, which is the ideal surface for a heavy coating of my spicy seasoning. Since I break them apart by hand, each piece is a totally different shape, with a different amount of skin, different surface-area-to-volume ratio, which makes the most delicious breakfast potato. In my opinion, the best dishes have a variety of textures, and with these, you get that variety in EVERY bite.

2 pounds russet potatoes, scrubbed

Kosher salt

1 teaspoon smoked paprika

1 teaspoon chili powder

1 teaspoon garlic powder

1 teaspoon onion powder

1 teaspoon cayenne pepper

1 teaspoon mustard powder

1 teaspoon celery salt

½ cup vegetable oil

1 green bell pepper, stemmed, seeded, and diced

1 medium yellow onion, diced

3 garlic cloves, chopped

Freshly ground black pepper

A few dashes of hot sauce, such as Cholula

1/ In a large pot, combine the potatoes, a generous amount of salt, and enough water to cover the potatoes. Bring to a boil over high heat, then reduce the heat to low and simmer until the potatoes are fork-tender, 20 to 30 minutes. Drain the potatoes and transfer them to a large bowl. Cool the potatoes completely, uncovered, ideally in the refrigerator overnight. (If you're cooking on the same day you plan to serve this, cool the potatoes for at least 2 hours in the refrigerator or 1 hour in the freezer.)

2/ While the potatoes are cooling, in a small bowl, combine the smoked paprika, chili powder, garlic powder, onion powder, cayenne, mustard powder, and celery salt.

3/ Remove the cooled potatoes from the refrigerator or freezer and use your hands to gently break them into rough, uneven pieces, about eight chunks per potato, about 2 inches or roughly the length of your thumb.

4/ Line a large heatproof bowl with paper towels. Heat a 12-inch cast-iron or stainless-steel skillet over medium heat and add the oil. Once it is shimmering, add half of the potatoes and cook, undisturbed, until deeply golden brown, about 2 minutes. Flip and repeat on the other side, cooking until deeply browned, another 2 minutes or so. Using a slotted spoon, transfer the potatoes to your prepared bowl. Repeat these steps with the remaining potatoes. Season immediately with salt and half of the spice mixture.

5/ Once all the potatoes are cooked, add the bell pepper and onion to the skillet. Season with salt and sauté until the bell pepper has softened and the onion is lightly browned, 4 to 5 minutes. Add the garlic and cook until fragrant, about 1 minute. Transfer the mixture to the bowl with the potatoes and sprinkle the remaining spice mixture evenly over the top, then stir to combine. Season to taste with salt and black pepper, drizzle with hot sauce, and serve immediately.

Coconut Yogurt Breakfast Ice Pops

● **MAKES 10 ICE POPS**

I've always loved coconut for its incredible flavor and versatility in both sweet and savory recipes. When a smoothie bowl shop opened near my house, I immediately went for their coconut bowl, and unsurprisingly I LOVED it. That said, I can't drive to their shop for that smoothie bowl every morning, so I realized I needed to re-create it at home.

The result of all those realizations, plus my desire to get more coconut in my life, is this ice pop recipe! Granola is probably the most surprising ingredient, but freezing it with the yogurt softens the texture on the outside, similar to what happens when you pour milk over cereal. You can mix in whatever fruit you have on hand (usually strawberries and blueberries for me), and because the yogurt is nondairy, these are good for all diets, including vegan ones. Best of all, I can make a big batch all at once, so in the morning I have breakfast ready, no dishes to do, and my coconut craving is satisfied in one ice pop.

1 cup coconut yogurt

1 (13.5-ounce) can full-fat coconut milk

¼ cup pure maple syrup

½ teaspoon pure vanilla extract

¼ teaspoon kosher salt

½ cup (about 4 ounces) stemmed and quartered strawberries

⅓ cup (about 2 ounces) blueberries

⅔ cup granola

SPECIAL EQUIPMENT

Ice pop mold and sticks

1/ In a medium bowl, whisk together the coconut yogurt, coconut milk, maple syrup, vanilla, and salt.

2/ Using a small spoon, add 2 or 3 quartered strawberry pieces to the bottom of ten ice pop molds. Pour about ¼ cup of the yogurt mixture into each mold, so that the mold is filled about two-thirds of the way. Press 2 or 3 blueberries in each mold, then sprinkle 1 tablespoon of the granola on top. Using your thumbs or the back of a spoon, lightly press the granola into the yogurt. Gently insert the sticks and freeze until set, at least 6 hours or overnight. (The ice pops will keep in the molds in the freezer for up to 3 months.)

QUICK BITE

This recipe is so, so customizable and flexible based on the ingredients you have (berries about to go bad), your favorite fruits (mango would be so good!), or whatever's in season. The options are truly limitless with this one!

Chilaquiles Rojos

● SERVES 5

I'm introducing this classic Mexican dish by talking about . . . a classic Jewish breakfast dish! Matzo brei is a dish we usually eat during Passover, and it's basically scrambled eggs and matzo (an unleavened bread, almost like a cracker) cooked together. The scrambled eggs are soft, the matzo is crunchy, and they make a pretty simple but delicious breakfast. In chilaquiles, tortilla chips get cooked in a perfectly spiced tomato sauce until they're soft but still have some tooth to them. You can make this dish even easier by doing parts of it—like making the red sauce—the day before. This is a dish I whip up when I want to impress my friends. It's jam-packed with flavor and super filling, and it makes a beautiful centerpiece on your breakfast table!

5 medium plum tomatoes, halved

4 tablespoons olive oil

1 medium white onion, chopped

4 garlic cloves, sliced

½ teaspoon ground cumin

2 tablespoons tomato paste

3 canned chipotle peppers in adobo

¼ cup chopped fresh cilantro, plus more for garnish

Kosher salt

4 large eggs

Freshly ground black pepper

8 ounces tortilla chips (about 8 cups)

Crumbled queso fresco and thin radish slices, for garnish

1/ Heat a large cast-iron skillet over high heat. Add the tomatoes, cut-side down, to the dry pan. Cook for 4 to 5 minutes, then flip and cook on the other side for 2 minutes, or until both sides are lightly charred. Transfer them to a large bowl and set aside.

2/ Heat 2 tablespoons of the olive oil in the same skillet over medium heat. Add the onion and cook until soft and translucent, about 5 minutes. Add the garlic and cumin and cook until fragrant, about 1 minute. Add the tomato paste and chipotles and cook until the mixture thickens and the tomato paste turns a darker brick red, stirring frequently, about 5 minutes. Turn off the heat and add 1 cup water to the pan, scraping any browned bits from the bottom.

3/ Transfer the mixture to a high-speed blender along with the tomatoes, cilantro, and a generous pinch of salt. Blend until smooth.

4/ Pour the blended tomato mixture back into the pan and simmer over medium-low heat until the mixture reduces slightly, about 10 minutes.

5/ While the tomato sauce simmers, heat the remaining 2 tablespoons olive oil in a large nonstick skillet over medium-high heat. Add the eggs (you might need to work in batches, depending on the size of your pan) and fry to the desired doneness, 5 minutes for a runny yolk and 8 minutes for a hard yolk, tilting the pan to the side and using a large spoon to baste the whites with the hot oil as you cook. Remove the pan from the heat and season the eggs with salt and black pepper.

6/ After the tomato mixture has simmered, remove it from the heat, add the chips, and stir to combine. Top with the fried eggs, then sprinkle cilantro, queso fresco, and radishes evenly over the top. Serve immediately.

Tex-Mex Breakfast Burrito

SERVES 4

For me, a great burrito must include four fundamentals: protein, starch, cheese, and salsa. So when I set out to make my breakfast burrito, I used this method as my guide. For a starch, I had to choose potatoes over rice (see page 41 for how much I *love* potatoes), and for protein, since it's the first meal of the day, why not double up on it? Eggs AND beans are a perfect match here, especially because they both come together super quickly. For the cheese, in a Tex-Mex burrito, the go-to is cheddar. Finally, I add my favorite homemade Pico de Gallo (see page 94), but your favorite store-bought salsa works just as well, and chopped avocado, because avocado makes everything better. And there you have it: the four essential components of a great burrito, breakfast edition.

2 medium russet potatoes (about 12 ounces), scrubbed

¼ cup plus 1 tablespoon vegetable oil

1 tablespoon garlic powder

1 tablespoon onion powder

1½ teaspoons dried oregano

½ teaspoon cayenne pepper

Kosher salt and freshly ground black pepper

3 large scallions, green and white parts, thinly sliced (optional)

6 large eggs, beaten

½ cup canned black beans, drained and rinsed

1 ripe avocado, chopped

1 cup grated sharp cheddar cheese

4 large flour tortillas

½ cup Pico de Gallo (page 94) or store-bought salsa, plus more for serving

Hot sauce and sour cream, for serving (optional)

1/ Using a box grater, grate the potatoes on the largest holes into a bowl, then transfer them to a clean kitchen towel and squeeze out any excess liquid. (Alternatively, you can grate them directly onto the kitchen towel.) Set aside.

2/ Heat ¼ cup of the oil in a large nonstick skillet set over medium-high heat. Add the potatoes and season with the garlic powder, onion powder, oregano, cayenne, salt, and black pepper. Arrange the potatoes in a single layer and cook undisturbed until golden brown, about 4 minutes. Flip to brown the other sides of the potatoes, another 4 minutes. Remove the cooked potatoes from the pan and set them aside. Remove the skillet from the heat and, when it's cool enough to touch, wipe it with a paper towel or kitchen towel to remove any remaining cooked bits.

3/ Using the same skillet, heat the remaining 1 tablespoon of oil over medium-low heat. Add the scallions, if using, and cook until softened, about

2 minutes. Add the eggs and scramble, cooking until set, as desired, about 2 minutes. Season with salt and black pepper. Remove the eggs from the skillet and set them aside.

4/ To assemble the burritos, evenly divide the potatoes, scrambled eggs, black beans, avocado, and cheese among 4 tortillas. (Do not add filling all the way to the edge of the tortilla.) Add 2 tablespoons of the Pico de Gallo to each burrito. Tuck in the sides and wrap it tightly.

5/ Wipe out the skillet and return it to the stovetop set over medium-low heat. Transfer the burritos to the skillet, seam-sides down, cover, and cook until golden brown on the outside, about 3 minutes per side. (You may need to work in batches, depending on the size of your skillet; keep cooked burritos warm under foil.) Serve immediately with more pico de gallo, as well as hot sauce and sour cream, if desired.

When I was developing this chapter, I spent a lot of time thinking about what I should call it and wondering what all these foods had in common. Finally, it hit me: I can eat them all with my favorite kitchen tool—my hands!

Although *handhelds* is a pretty loose term, and you'll find a lot of different types of food in this chapter, one thing I love about these recipes is that they're all pretty casual. There are a wide variety of dishes here and nothing that has to be eaten at a certain meal or time of day—you don't even have to be sitting down to enjoy them! Another thing that most of these recipes have in common is that they feature my all-time favorite food group: CARBS! And like most carb-forward foods, the sauces and accompaniments really make the dish. For example, some of the most famous kinds of handhelds are street foods: quick to assemble and easy to eat on the move—and the **Chicken Kathi Rolls** (page 66) are just that. Of course, another classic handheld is a sandwich, and what's more classic than a grilled cheese? Some say you can't improve on a sandwich this iconic, but I add a **Blueberry-Thyme Jam** (page 51) to mine that cuts through the salt and fat of the cheese and balances the sandwich perfectly. Finally, I would be remiss if I didn't mention tacos and burgers! Since I firmly believe you cannot have too many of either of these, I've included recipes for two flavor-packed variations of each. I'd recommend you get plenty of napkins ready before you dive into this chapter!

HANDHELDS

Double Grilled Cheese

WITH BLUEBERRY-THYME JAM

● **MAKES 4 SANDWICHES**

Watch out, grilled cheeses of the world! This recipe is going to put you all to shame! Now, you may be thinking, *Hold up, Eitan, there's jam inside this grilled cheese?* And to that I say, YES! Yes, there is! The jam layer adds sweetness, and that, combined with a little acidity from the lemon, pairs perfectly with the fatty, melty cheese.

As for the cheese, this sandwich packs a punch, with Gouda on the inside and the outside slathered with mayo (mayo > butter!) *and* a slice of good old American cheese. American gets the exterior crispier than regular bread and butter ever could, which contrasts with the jammy, gooey Gouda interior in a complex, insanely delectable way. Make this for someone you want to impress, and get ready for the cheese pull before you dig in!

BLUEBERRY-THYME JAM
2 cups fresh blueberries
⅓ cup sugar
Juice of 1 lemon
5 fresh thyme sprigs

¼ teaspoon kosher salt

GRILLED CHEESE
Mayonnaise
8 (½-inch-thick) slices sourdough bread

4 slices American cheese, plus more as needed to cover the bread
1 pound Gouda cheese, cut into ¼-inch-thick slices

1/ MAKE THE JAM In a medium saucepot, combine 1¼ cups of the blueberries, sugar, and lemon juice and bring to a boil over medium-high heat. Stirring occasionally, being sure to scrape the bottom and sides of the pot, boil the mixture vigorously for 10 minutes, or until the jam has reduced by three-quarters. Reduce the heat to medium and add the remaining ¾ cup blueberries, the thyme, and the salt. Stir to combine and cook for an additional 5 minutes. Remove from the heat and let cool slightly. Remove the thyme sprigs, then pour the jam into a heatproof resealable jar and cool to room temperature. Cover and refrigerate until you are ready to make the sandwiches.

2/ MAKE THE GRILLED CHEESE Spread a thin layer of mayonnaise on one side of each of the bread slices. Cover the mayonnaise side with a layer of American cheese, making sure the entire surface of the bread is covered (you may need more than one slice, depending on the size of

your bread). Flip all of the bread slices cheese-side-down, then spread a thin layer of jam on four bread slices.

3/ Set a large nonstick skillet over medium-low heat. Once the skillet is hot, working with two sandwiches at a time, add 2 slices of bread without jam to the skillet, cheese-side down.

4/ Place one-quarter of the sliced Gouda on each sandwich, then top each with a jam-coated slice of bread, jam-side facing down. Cook until the American cheese is bubbling and browned, 4 to 5 minutes. Carefully flip the sandwiches and repeat on the other side, cooking another 4 to 5 minutes. Repeat for the remaining 2 sandwiches.

5/ Transfer the sandwiches to a cutting board and cut each sandwich in half. Serve immediately.

Garlic Naan

● MAKES 8 TO 10 NAAN

True story: I once campaigned hard for my parents to install a tandoor oven in our kitchen. I'm sad to report I was not successful, *but* this meant that I was forced to figure out how to make exceptional naan without one, and after you try this recipe, you can, too. A tandoor is a cylinder-shaped oven made of brick and clay that cooks food with direct, intense heat, similar to a pizza oven. When naan is placed in a tandoor, it cooks directly on the oven wall—one side of the bread sticks to the tandoor, giving it a slight crunch, and the other side, exposed to the direct flame, gets smoky charred bits. I developed a method where you stick the dough to a super-hot pan (this is your tandoor oven wall!), then flip the dough upside down so that the top is exposed to some direct heat (this is your open flame!). Don't worry: If that sounds intimidating (or if you are cooking on an electric cooktop), I've included an alternative method, which requires zero flipping or open flames and is equally delicious, I promise.

2 cups (473g) warm water (about 100°F)

2 tablespoons sugar

2 (0.25-ounce) packets active dry yeast

5 cups (560g) all-purpose flour, plus more for dusting

2 teaspoons kosher salt

¼ cup (61g) whole-milk plain, or coconut yogurt

½ stick (55g) unsalted butter or vegan butter, melted, or ¼ cup ghee, plus more as needed

6 garlic cloves, finely chopped

½ cup fresh cilantro, chopped

1/ In a small bowl, mix together the warm water and sugar until fully dissolved. Sprinkle the yeast over the water and let sit until foamy, 5 to 10 minutes.

2/ In a large bowl, mix the flour and salt until fully combined. Add the yeast mixture and yogurt to the flour, then mix it all together with a wooden spoon until it begins to form a shaggy ball of dough.

3/ Transfer the dough to a lightly floured work surface and knead with your hands until smooth, about 5 minutes. Place the dough in a greased bowl, cover with plastic wrap, and let it rise until doubled in size, about 1 hour, then punch it down to release the air. Place the dough on a lightly floured work surface and cut it into 8 to 10 portions. Shape each portion into a ball, then, on a lightly floured surface, use a rolling pin to carefully roll each one into a 4 × 6-inch oval, about ¼ inch thick.

4/ Heat a large skillet or tawa (the pan cannot have a nonstick coating; see Quick Bite) over high heat, until it is very hot, about 2 minutes. Brush one piece of dough with water, then transfer it to the hot skillet, water-side

down. Let the naan cook until the edges become opaque and bubbles form on the cooked side, 30 to 45 seconds, then flip the whole pan upside down (the dough should stick to the pan) and cook it over the direct flame for 1 to 2 minutes, checking every few seconds to ensure even cooking and browning. (Alternatively, brush one side of a piece of dough with melted butter or ghee.) Place the dough butter-side down in the pan and cook for 1 minute, or until large bubbles form on the top. Flip and cook the other side for about 45 seconds.

5/ Remove the naan, brush it with melted butter or ghee, and top with garlic and cilantro. Repeat with the remaining naan. Serve hot.

QUICK BITE

This method won't work in pans with a nonstick coating, so it's really important that you use one without it, such as a stainless-steel pan. When you wet the bottom of the dough, the starch in the dough combines with the water, creating a glue-like seal that allows the dough to stick to the hot pan, so you can flip the pan upside down without the naan falling off!

Beef Souvlaki

WITH TZATZIKI

● SERVES 6 TO 8

Souvlaki is a popular Greek fast food made by marinating chunks of meat in oil, lemon juice, and oregano, then skewering and grilling them. The word *souvlaki* simply means "meat on skewers," and it is indeed usually eaten right off that skewer, though it can also be served in pita with fresh lemon and various sauces. Traditionally, it's made with pork, but lamb, beef, and chicken are also very common and equally delicious. Souvlaki is smoky and savory, so tzatziki, which is bright, herbaceous, and packed with cucumber and dill, is the perfect complement. This recipe, which uses beef, is especially good when you are short on prep time, because the meat and sauce can be made hours in advance. The toppings can be assembled in the time it takes to grill the beef, which means this dinner is cooked and on the table in under thirty minutes!

BEEF SKEWERS

2 pounds steak, such as sirloin or New York strip, at least 1½ inches thick

½ cup olive oil

2 tablespoons minced garlic

2 tablespoons fresh oregano leaves, or 1 tablespoon dried

Juice of 1 lemon

Kosher salt and freshly ground black pepper

TZATZIKI

1½ cups plain yogurt (I use nondairy coconut yogurt)

½ cup diced cucumber

1 tablespoon minced garlic

2 tablespoons olive oil

1 tablespoon red wine vinegar

1 tablespoon chopped fresh dill

1 tablespoon chopped fresh mint

2 teaspoons lemon juice

Kosher salt and freshly ground black pepper

Pita bread, for serving (optional)

1/ **MAKE THE BEEF SKEWERS** Cut the steak into 1- to 1½-inch cubes. Place the steak, olive oil, garlic, oregano, and lemon juice in a large resealable bag and shake to combine the marinade with the beef. Transfer the bag to the refrigerator and marinate for at least 2 hours or up to overnight.

2/ **MAKE THE TZATZIKI** While the steak is marinating, combine all the ingredients in a medium bowl, adding salt and pepper to taste, and mix until well blended. Refrigerate until ready to serve.

3/ To cook the skewers, preheat a grill or grill pan to medium-high heat. Thread the steak pieces onto skewers (discarding the marinade) and season with salt and pepper.

Grill until nicely browned all over, 10 to 11 minutes, rotating throughout to ensure even cooking.

4/ Serve the souvlaki hot with pita (if desired) and tzatziki on the side.

QUICK BITE

If you don't have an outdoor grill or a grill pan for your stovetop, the best way to get a similar char and flavor is by cooking the meat under the broiler. To do this, place the skewers on a sheet pan and adjust a rack one-quarter of the way from the top of the oven. Broil on high for 10 to 15 minutes, turning often, until the meat reaches the desired doneness and is slightly charred around the edges.

Out-n-In Burger

● MAKES 4 BURGERS

Inspired by the Animal Style burgers of the iconic California fast-food chain In-N-Out Burger, this recipe delivers everything you could ever want in a cheeseburger and is worth the couple of extra steps it takes to build them.

Let's start with the most important part: the sauce, which is actually a very classic fry sauce. What I love about fry sauce is that it's just a combination of other great sauces that most of us have in our refrigerators. My version is a mix of ketchup, mustard, relish, and hot sauce to add tang, spice, sweetness . . . and messiness. The cheese *has* to be classic American; no cheese is creamier or melts better, and it really helps hold the burger together. Finally, the one thing that CANNOT be rushed or skipped in this recipe is the caramelized onions. The depth of flavor that develops from the low-and-slow cooking process takes this burger above and beyond. I'd recommend a short-sleeve shirt and a bunch of napkins for eating one of these; they are insanely delicious!

CARAMELIZED ONIONS

3 tablespoons unsalted butter

2 large onions, chopped (about 4 cups)

Kosher salt

Freshly ground black pepper

SAUCE

¼ cup mayonnaise

¼ cup ketchup

¼ cup finely chopped dill pickles

½ teaspoon yellow mustard

1 teaspoon apple cider vinegar

¼ teaspoon sugar

2 dashes of hot sauce

Kosher salt and freshly ground black pepper

BURGERS

1 pound ground protein (I use plant-based protein)

Kosher salt and freshly ground black pepper

1 tablespoon vegetable oil, for frying

ASSEMBLY

4 slices American cheese

4 hamburger buns, lightly toasted

Iceberg lettuce, shredded

1 beefsteak tomato, sliced

Dill pickles, sliced

1/ **CARAMELIZE THE ONIONS** In a large skillet, melt the butter over medium heat. Add the onions and a pinch of salt and cook, stirring often, until they caramelize and turn a deep golden-brown color, 20 to 25 minutes. Season to taste with salt and pepper and set aside.

2/ **MAKE THE SAUCE** In a small bowl, combine all the ingredients, adding salt and pepper to taste, and mix until well blended. Keep refrigerated until the burgers are ready. (Leftover sauce can be stored in the refrigerator for up to 1 week.)

3/ **MAKE THE BURGERS** Divide the ground protein into 4 equal 4-ounce portions. Shape them into 4-inch patties (about ½ inch thick) and make a slight

indentation in the center with your thumb. Season assertively with salt and pepper on both sides.

4/ Preheat a large skillet over medium-high heat and add the oil. Once the oil is shimmering, add the patties and sear them until deeply golden brown, 2 minutes per side for medium-rare, or 3 to 4 minutes per side for medium-well. Top each patty with a slice of cheese, remove the pan from the heat, cover, and let melt, about 1 minute.

5/ Transfer the patties to the lightly toasted buns and top with the caramelized onions, sauce, lettuce, tomato, and pickles.

Arayes
WITH ISRAELI PITA

● SERVES 8 AS AN ENTRÉE
OR 16 AS AN APPETIZER

Arayes are essentially a kebab cooked inside a pita to create one delectable package. The filling is traditionally made with ground beef or lamb, and I personally prefer beef. The meat mixture is loaded with flavor: onion, garlic, fresh herbs, lemon, lots of spices, and, most important to me, toasted pine nuts. Arayes are found all over the Middle East, but this recipe is based on the Israeli version that utilizes a thicker pita, making it a more sandwich-like recipe. If you want an idea of *why* these pitas are so delicious, it's because all the flavorful juices from cooking the seasoned meat are absorbed by the pita, instead of dripping and disappearing in the grill. No precious flavor left behind!

MEAT-STUFFED PITAS

2 pounds (80/20) ground beef
   or ground lamb

1 red onion, cut into large wedges

4 garlic cloves, crushed

½ cup fresh parsley leaves

½ cup fresh cilantro leaves

2 tablespoons lemon juice

1 tablespoon ground cumin

2 teaspoons kosher salt

1 teaspoon freshly ground
   black pepper

1 teaspoon cayenne pepper

½ teaspoon ground allspice

½ teaspoon ground cinnamon

¼ cup toasted pine nuts (optional)

8 pitas, preferably Israeli, cut in half
   (see Quick Bite)

1 tablespoon olive oil, plus more
   if needed

TAHINI SAUCE

⅓ cup well-stirred tahini

2 tablespoons lemon juice

1 teaspoon ground cumin

Kosher salt

1/ MAKE THE PITAS Remove the ground beef from the refrigerator to let it come toward room temperature, about 30 minutes.

2/ Add the onion to the bowl of a food processor and pulse for 10 to 15 seconds, scraping down the sides of the bowl between pulses, if needed. Then add the garlic, parsley, and cilantro and process for 30 to 45 seconds, until the mixture is finely ground. Transfer the mixture to a large bowl along with the beef, lemon juice, cumin, salt, black pepper, cayenne, allspice, cinnamon, and pine nuts (if using). Gently stir the mixture to incorporate all ingredients. Using clean hands, gently open the "pocket" of each pita half without tearing the pita and fill it with about ½ cup of the meat mixture.

3/ In a large grill pan or skillet set over medium heat, add the olive oil. Place one batch of pitas cut-side down, so the meat is touching the skillet, and cook until the meat is crisp and dark golden brown, 5 to 7 minutes. Flip the pitas onto one side and cook bread-side down for 2 minutes, then flip once more and cook the second side

for an additional 2 minutes, or until the meat reaches the desired degree of doneness. Remove from the heat and cook the rest of the batches, adding additional oil if needed.

4/ MAKE THE TAHINI SAUCE In a small serving bowl, add the tahini. Slowly whisk in ⅓ cup cold water and the lemon juice until the ingredients are fully combined and the sauce has a thin, pourable consistency. Add the cumin and whisk once more to combine. Taste, season with salt, then whisk once more. Serve the pitas warm, with tahini sauce on the side.

QUICK BITE
Israeli pita is thicker and spongier than grocery pita, so I call for it here because it stands up better to filling and cooking. (You can find it at Middle Eastern grocery stores and online.) But if you can't track it down, any grocery store pita will work. Just reduce the filling in each pita to ⅓ cup, and be extra careful when you cook it that the pita doesn't break!

Chicken Satay
WITH PEANUT SAUCE

● SERVES 4

My mom taught me how to make chicken satay years ago, and it's been a favorite in our house ever since. Satay is a Southeast Asian dish of skewered meat that is marinated, grilled, and served with a dipping sauce. At food stalls on the streets of Thailand, Indonesia, Malaysia, and elsewhere in the region, you can find vendors grilling these skewers over hot coals. There are lots of regional variations, and this version consists of flavorful chicken that takes on a beautiful bright yellow color thanks to the turmeric in the marinade. This dish makes for a delicious appetizer, but it can easily become part of a full meal with a side dish or two!

CHICKEN SATAY

1 cup full-fat (not lite) coconut milk

Juice of 1 lime

2 tablespoons soy sauce

2 tablespoons light brown sugar

1 tablespoon chopped fresh cilantro

1 teaspoon sriracha

1 teaspoon ground turmeric

1 teaspoon grated garlic (from 2 cloves)

1 teaspoon grated ginger (from a 1-inch piece of fresh ginger)

1 teaspoon kosher salt, plus more as needed

¼ teaspoon freshly ground black pepper, plus more as needed

2 pounds skinless, boneless chicken breasts (about 4 breasts), cut lengthwise into ½-inch strips

PEANUT SAUCE

½ cup creamy peanut butter

½ cup full-fat coconut milk

2 tablespoons soy sauce

1 tablespoon sriracha

1 tablespoon toasted sesame oil

1 tablespoon fresh lime juice

2 teaspoons light brown sugar

1 small garlic clove, grated

1 teaspoon grated ginger (from a 1-inch piece of fresh ginger)

¼ cup chopped peanuts

SERVING

Fresh cilantro leaves, whole or chopped

Crushed red pepper flakes

Chopped peanuts

1/ MARINATE THE CHICKEN SATAY In a large bowl, combine the coconut milk, lime juice, soy sauce, brown sugar, cilantro, sriracha, turmeric, garlic, ginger, salt, and pepper and mix until well combined. Add the chicken, toss to coat, then cover and chill in the refrigerator for at least 1 or up to 4 hours.

2/ MAKE THE PEANUT SAUCE In a medium bowl, combine the peanut butter, coconut milk, soy sauce, sriracha, sesame oil, lime juice, brown sugar, garlic, and ginger and whisk until fully combined. Add the chopped peanuts and stir until incorporated.

3/ Preheat a gas grill to medium. Thread two pieces of chicken onto a wooden skewer and repeat with the remaining chicken. Season with salt and pepper. Grill the skewers until browned, with grill marks on both sides,

6 to 7 minutes per side. (Alternatively, place a lightly oiled grill pan on the stovetop over medium heat. Grill the skewers until cooked through, 4 to 5 minutes per side.) Top with cilantro, red pepper flakes, and peanuts and serve with the peanut sauce on the side.

QUICK BITE

Important note! For all the recipes in this book that involve a marinated protein (such as this recipe or the Beef Souvlaki with Tzatziki on page 55), the marinating time doesn't have to be exactly what's written in the recipe. In most cases, the longer you marinate the protein, the better the final dish will be since it becomes more flavorful. However, if you are short on time, you can marinate for as much time as you have, even if that's just 15 to 30 minutes. The results might be less flavorful, but they will still be delicious.

Bánh Mì-Style Tofu Sandwich

● **MAKES 4 SANDWICHES**

Bánh mì is the Vietnamese word for "bread," but it is most often associated with a crispy-on-the-outside, soft-and-chewy-on-the-inside loaf, similar to a baguette, and the tasty sandwiches that are made with it. Typical bánh mì fillings combine a mix of Vietnamese ingredients, like cilantro and daikon, with French ones, such as pâté and mayonnaise. However, possibilities for variations are endless, and in this recipe, I substitute tofu for the meat and steep it in a super-quick, high-flavor marinade. The tofu soaks up the marinade like a sponge, so when it's seared, the sugars from the marinade caramelize to add yet another layer of flavor, as well as a layer of texture: a crispy outside and a soft, almost creamy interior. The pickled vegetables add vital crunch and bright acidity, and the spicy mayo rounds out the tastes and textures with creaminess and a little heat.

PICKLED VEGGIES

1 (2-inch) piece daikon radish, peeled and cut into matchsticks

2 small carrots, cut into matchsticks

1 small Persian cucumber, cut into matchsticks

1 jalapeño, thinly sliced

1 cup rice wine vinegar

1 tablespoon sugar

1 tablespoon kosher salt

TOFU

1 (15-ounce) block extra-firm tofu, drained

¼ cup soy sauce or tamari

2 tablespoons hoisin sauce

2 tablespoons toasted sesame oil

1 large garlic clove, grated

1 (1-inch) piece fresh ginger, peeled and grated

Juice of 1 lime

1 tablespoon vegetable oil

SRIRACHA MAYO

½ cup mayonnaise

¼ cup sriracha

ASSEMBLY

1 large baguette, heels removed and sliced into 4 pieces

2 cups loosely packed fresh cilantro leaves and stems

1 / MAKE THE PICKLED VEGGIES Place the daikon, carrots, cucumbers, and jalapeño in a medium jar with the rice vinegar, sugar, and salt. If the veggies are not submerged in the vinegar, add enough water to cover them. Cover, shake the jar to marry the ingredients, place in the refrigerator, and chill for at least 1 hour.

2 / MARINATE THE TOFU Wrap the tofu block in paper towels and place it on a sheet pan. Set something heavy on top, like a cast-iron skillet or a pan weighted with cans. Let drain for at least 15 minutes or up to 1 hour. Slice the tofu lengthwise into ½-inch-thick planks.

3 / In a shallow bowl, combine the soy sauce, hoisin, toasted sesame oil, garlic, ginger, and lime juice. Add the tofu and coat completely in marinade. Let marinate at room temperature for 15 minutes.

4 / MAKE THE SRIRACHA MAYO In a medium bowl, stir together the mayonnaise and sriracha and set aside.

5 / COOK THE TOFU Heat a nonstick skillet over medium-high heat. Add the vegetable oil to the pan and arrange the tofu in an even layer (reserve the marinade). Cook undisturbed until golden brown and caramelized on the bottom, 2 to 3 minutes, then flip and cook the other side. Return the cooked tofu pieces to the marinade.

6 / ASSEMBLE THE SANDWICHES Slice each piece of baguette in half lengthwise. Liberally spread the sriracha mayo on all eight cut sides of the bread, followed by some of the pickled veggies on one half and cilantro on the other. Top the pickled-veggie side with the tofu, drizzle a few tablespoons of the reserved marinade over, then cover with the other bread half and serve.

Chicken Kathi Rolls

● MAKES 8 ROLLS

To fully appreciate any cuisine, you have to get to know its street food. I first learned about kathi rolls while watching a documentary about the cuisine of Kolkata, one of India's biggest cities. I went to the kitchen immediately to try to re-create them and have been obsessed ever since. Kathi rolls hit all the great street food notes (portable, filling, flavorful) and are made by vendors across the city every day, often late into the night. Traditional fillings include beef, mutton, potato, and chicken. Shredded chicken is covered in a mix of warm spices and cooked, then piled into a roti (an Indian flatbread). The roti is lined with scrambled eggs and topped with red onion, tamarind chutney, cilantro, and mint chutney. All rolled up into the perfect grab-and-go meal, it's packed with all the flavors I love about Indian cuisine in a handheld, easy-to-eat package.

ROTI

2 cups whole wheat flour, preferably atta or finely ground whole wheat flour (see Quick Bite), plus more for dusting

¾ teaspoon kosher salt

1½ tablespoons vegetable oil

CHICKEN

2 tablespoons vegetable oil

2 teaspoons whole cumin seeds

1 large yellow onion, chopped

3 garlic cloves, minced

½-inch piece fresh ginger, peeled and grated

1 teaspoon chili powder

1 teaspoon ground coriander

1 teaspoon ground turmeric

Kosher salt and freshly ground black pepper

2 cups shredded rotisserie chicken or shredded cooked chicken (see page 157)

½ cup chicken stock or water

ASSEMBLY

8 large eggs

Nonstick cooking spray

Tamarind Chutney (page 112)

1 small red onion, thinly sliced

Fresh cilantro leaves, for garnish

Mint Chutney (page 108)

1/ **MAKE THE ROTI** In a large bowl, mix the flour and salt together. Add the vegetable oil and mix with your fingers until it is fully combined. Slowly add ¾ cup water, while continuing to mix until a soft ball of dough forms. Knead the dough on a lightly floured surface until it is smooth and elastic and does not resist much when pushed with a finger, 2 to 3 minutes. Cover with plastic wrap and let rest for 10 minutes.

2/ Line a sheet pan with parchment paper. Set aside.

3/ Cut the rested dough into 8 equal pieces and roll each into golf-ball-size balls. Cover the dough balls lightly with plastic wrap to prevent them from drying out. Working with one piece of dough on a lightly floured surface, roll out each piece to ⅛-inch thickness and transfer it to the parchment-lined sheet pan. Repeat with the remaining dough, stacking the roti on top of each

other and separating them with a layer of parchment paper in between.

4/ Preheat a cast-iron skillet, large frying pan, or an Indian tawa over medium-high heat and, when hot, cook one roti at a time until the edges are opaque, 1 to 2 minutes, then flip and cook the other side for another minute or two. (The dough should puff up and be lightly browned on both sides.) Repeat with the remaining roti, then set them aside while you prepare the chicken.

5/ **MAKE THE CHICKEN** In a large skillet, heat the vegetable oil over medium heat. Add the cumin seeds, stir immediately, and cook for 1 to 2 minutes, until aromatic. Lower the heat to medium-low, add the onion, garlic, and ginger, and cook over medium-low heat until the edges begin to brown, 3 to 4 minutes. Add the chili powder, coriander, turmeric, and salt and pepper to taste. Cook for an additional minute, until aromatic, then stir in the chicken and chicken stock. Raise the heat to medium-high and cook for 2 to 3 minutes, until most of the stock is evaporated. Remove from the heat and set aside.

6/ TO ASSEMBLE Beat the eggs together in a large glass measuring cup (at least 2 cups in volume) with a spout. Spray an 8- or 9-inch nonstick skillet with cooking spray, then place the skillet over medium-low heat. Add about ¼ cup of the beaten egg mixture and top with one roti. Cook for 1 to 2 minutes, until the egg is set. Remove from the pan, flip, then top the egg with 1 teaspoon of the tamarind chutney, spreading it into an even layer. Add ¼ cup of the cooked chicken mixture, a few slices of red onion, some fresh cilantro, and a drizzle of mint chutney. Roll it up into a tight spiral. Repeat with the remaining roti.

QUICK BITE

For this recipe, I went with chicken for the filling, but feel free to switch it up with whatever you'd like. You can use beef, lamb, paneer cheese, or any other flavorful filling you want. Kathi rolls are always my go-to whenever I have leftover meat in the house, because they turn last night's dinner into a delicious treat. For the roti, you can use regular whole wheat flour, but atta or a more finely ground whole wheat flour will give you the best texture. I use Sujata Gold Atta, which is available online.

Beer-Battered Wild Mushroom Tacos

Let's start this recipe by establishing that I absolutely love mushrooms. What can I say? I'm a FUN GUY who loves FUNGI! When I was trying to figure out how to get my beloved 'shrooms into a taco, I was super inspired by Baja fish tacos, which usually include some kind of beer-battered fish. I know that deep-frying can seem like a daunting process, but if you follow the tips in my Quick Bite, it's just as straightforward as any other cooking method, and the shatteringly crisp mushrooms are totally worth it.

● SERVES 4 TO 6

AVOCADO CREMA

2 ripe avocados

¼ cup plain full-fat Greek yogurt or sour cream

¼ cup fresh cilantro leaves

Zest and juice of 1 lime

1 garlic clove, grated

Honey

Kosher salt and freshly ground black pepper

TACOS

1 cup all-purpose flour

1 tablespoon garlic powder

1 teaspoon kosher salt, plus more as needed

½ teaspoon smoked paprika

¼ teaspoon cayenne pepper

Freshly ground black pepper

1¼ cups light beer

Vegetable oil, for frying

10 ounces oyster mushrooms, torn into 2-inch pieces

SERVING

12 to 16 (8-inch) corn tortillas

Iceberg lettuce, shredded

Pico de Gallo (page 94) or store-bought salsa

Hot sauce (optional)

1/ **MAKE THE CREMA** In the bowl of a food processor or blender, add the flesh of the avocados, yogurt, cilantro, lime zest and juice, and garlic and process until well combined. Stream in ¼ cup cold water, adding more as needed, until it's thinned to the desired consistency. Taste, and if the mixture is too acidic, drizzle in a bit of honey. Season with salt and pepper and blend again. Transfer to a container and refrigerate.

2/ **MAKE THE TACOS** In a large bowl, whisk together the flour, garlic powder, salt, smoked paprika, cayenne, and black pepper. Add the beer and whisk to combine.

3/ Fill a large Dutch oven with 1½ inches of oil and heat over medium heat until the oil reaches 350°F (see Quick Bite). Line a sheet pan with paper towels and place it nearby. Working in batches and using tongs, dip each mushroom into the beer batter, let the excess batter drip off, then carefully lower it into the hot oil. (The oil should bubble as soon as the mushroom is placed in it.) Cook

until golden brown, flipping with tongs halfway through, about 3 minutes per side. Using tongs, transfer the mushrooms to the prepared sheet pan. Season with salt immediately and repeat with the remaining mushrooms.

4/ To assemble the tacos, heat the tortillas directly over a gas burner until toasted and charred in places, about 30 seconds, or place them on a sheet pan and warm under a broiler set to low, 1 to 2 minutes. Top the tortillas with fried mushrooms, lettuce, pico de gallo, avocado crema, and hot sauce (if using), and serve.

QUICK BITE

Don't be daunted by deep-frying! 1) Keep your pot on a back burner. (The farther it is from the edge of your stove, the better!) 2) Never fill your pot more than halfway with oil, and make sure you let the oil cool fully before you dispose of it. 3) Use an instant-read thermometer (or deep-frying thermometer) so you always know the exact oil temperature!

Croque Monsieur Tuna Melt

● MAKES 4 SANDWICHES

This recipe is the perfect example of me doing one of my favorite culinary activities: Take a classic comfort food that you can find on any diner menu—the beloved tuna melt—and make it just a little bit fancy, in this case by giving it a French "croque monsieur" treatment.

A traditional croque monsieur is a broiled or grilled ham, cheese, and béchamel sandwich. Instead of ham, I substitute tuna salad, which is actually a great candidate for some classic French flavors, since it often has pickles and mustard in it already. Next, a tuna melt's usual American cheese gets swapped for a delicious Mornay sauce (think béchamel, but with cheese added) and is piled with even more salty, creamy Gruyère before a final broil in the oven for maximum gooeyness. If you already love a tuna melt, this extra cheesy, extra fancy version will be your new favorite!

TUNA SALAD

3 (6-ounce) cans solid white tuna packed in water, drained

⅓ cup mayonnaise

2 tablespoons Dijon mustard

2 tablespoons lemon juice

1 teaspoon dried dill

¼ cup finely chopped shallot

¼ cup finely chopped celery

¼ cup finely chopped cornichons

Kosher salt and freshly black ground pepper

MORNAY SAUCE

2 tablespoons unsalted butter

2 tablespoons all-purpose flour

1½ cups whole milk

½ cup grated Gruyère cheese

Kosher salt and freshly ground black pepper

ASSEMBLY

8 (½-inch-thick) slices bread, such as sourdough, toasted

Dijon mustard

1¼ cups grated Gruyère cheese

1/ Preheat the oven to 400°F and place a rack in the upper third.

2/ **MAKE THE TUNA SALAD** Place the tuna in a fine-mesh sieve. Using the back of a wooden spoon or large serving spoon, press out any excess moisture, ensuring the tuna is as dry as possible. Set aside.

3/ Place the mayonnaise, mustard, lemon juice, and dill in a large bowl and whisk to combine. Add the shallot, celery, and cornichons to the bowl and whisk again to combine. Add the tuna and stir until just mixed. Taste and season with salt and pepper and set aside.

4/ **MAKE THE MORNAY SAUCE** In a medium saucepan over medium heat, melt the butter. Once the butter is fully melted, sprinkle the flour evenly over it and, whisking vigorously, cook until it smells nutty, 1 to 2 minutes. Slowly pour in the milk, whisking constantly to prevent lumps. Cook, stirring constantly, until the sauce thickens, 3 to 5 minutes. (If the mixture climbs above a simmer, reduce the heat to medium-low.) The sauce should coat the back of a wooden spoon, and a clean line should hold when you drag a finger across it. Remove from the heat and whisk in the Gruyère until fully incorporated. Stir in the salt and pepper to taste, then set aside until ready to use.

5/ **ASSEMBLE THE SANDWICHES** Arrange 4 slices of toasted bread on a sheet pan and spread mustard on top. Divide the tuna salad among the 4 slices, then top each with ¼ cup of the grated Gruyère. Place the remaining toasts on top, then pour the sauce evenly over the sandwiches. Sprinkle the remaining ¼ cup grated Gruyère over the sandwiches, place them in the oven, and bake for 5 minutes. Turn the oven to low broil and broil until the cheese is melted and the sauce is bubbling and browned, 2 to 3 minutes more. Let cool slightly before cutting each sandwich in half. Serve immediately.

Bruschetta Avocado Toast

● MAKES 4 SLICES

When I was coming up with the recipes for this book, I knew I wanted to do bruschetta, *and* I knew I wanted to do avocado toast. And then I thought, *What's better than one kind of topping on bread?* TWO! And, thus, this bruschetta avocado toast was born. The finished dish is a raging flavor and texture party: the crunchy toast, creamy and mild avocado mash, and vinegary, garlicky bruschetta all mingling together. I love how the vinaigrette drips down and flavors everything below it, and because the bread is lightly fried in olive oil, it can absorb the dressing without getting soggy or falling apart. After one bite, you might wonder why these two beloved toast toppings haven't been combined before. This snack is truly a match made in heaven!

BRUSCHETTA

3 Roma tomatoes, chopped

⅓ cup chopped red onion (about ½ small onion)

1 garlic clove, minced

2 tablespoons balsamic vinegar

1 tablespoon extra-virgin olive oil

¼ cup packed basil leaves, torn into bite-size pieces

Kosher salt and freshly ground black pepper

AVOCADO MASH

3 ripe avocados, peeled and pitted

¼ cup packed basil leaves, torn into bite-size pieces

Zest and juice of 1 lemon

Kosher salt and freshly ground black pepper

ASSEMBLY

4 tablespoons olive oil

4 (1-inch-thick) slices sourdough bread

1/ **MAKE THE BRUSCHETTA** In a medium bowl, combine all the ingredients, adding salt and pepper to taste, and stir until well blended.

2/ **MAKE THE AVOCADO MASH** In a separate medium bowl, combine all the ingredients, adding salt and pepper to taste, and mash until well blended.

3/ In a large skillet set over medium heat, add 2 tablespoons of the oil. When the oil is hot and shimmering, add 2 slices of the bread and sauté on both sides until golden brown, about 60 to 90 seconds on each side. Transfer the fried bread to a serving platter. Add the remaining 2 tablespoons oil to the skillet and repeat with the remaining 2 bread slices.

4/ Divide the avocado mixture among the 4 toasts, spreading it to coat the surface area of the bread. Top each toast with a few spoonfuls of the bruschetta mixture and serve immediately.

Mushroom Philly Cheesesteaks

● MAKES 4 SANDWICHES

During a trip to Philly, I happened to walk by a vegetarian restaurant that served Philly cheesesteak. I did a double take, then headed inside. I love recipes that use vegetables to make popular meat dishes into equally great vegetarian versions. I ate every bite and didn't miss the steak *at all.* The key to mimicking the texture of the steak is to use a mix of different mushrooms. The different shapes and densities give the same bite and heft as meat when they're cooked. All the mushroom deliciousness gets piled into a warm hoagie roll, covered in provolone cheese, and broiled to bubbly, gooey sandwich perfection.

---

8 tablespoons vegetable oil

3 pounds mixed mushrooms (such as shiitake, oyster, cremini, and maitake), stemmed and thickly sliced

Kosher salt and freshly ground black pepper

2 green bell peppers, thinly sliced

1 medium onion, thinly sliced

3 garlic cloves, chopped

3 tablespoons tomato paste

¼ cup oil-packed sun-dried tomatoes, drained and chopped

1 cup vegetable stock

3 tablespoons soy sauce

2 tablespoons balsamic vinegar

1 tablespoon fresh lemon juice

1 teaspoon Dijon mustard

1 teaspoon onion powder

1 teaspoon garlic powder

½ teaspoon sugar

SERVING

4 (10- to 12-inch) hoagie rolls

16 slices provolone cheese, preferably sharp

1/ In a large skillet set over medium-high heat, add 2 tablespoons of the vegetable oil. Once the oil is hot and shimmering, add one-third of the sliced mushrooms. Cook, stirring occasionally, until the mushrooms are golden brown and crisp on the edges, about 6 minutes. Remove the mushrooms from the pan to a large bowl and season with salt and pepper. Repeat the process, adding 2 tablespoons of the oil for each batch.

2/ Using the same skillet set over medium-high heat, add the remaining 2 tablespoons of oil, then stir in the bell peppers and onion. Season with salt and pepper. Cook until the vegetables begin to brown around the edges, 4 to 5 minutes, then stir in ¼ cup water. Cook until the vegetables are caramelized and softened, adding more water if needed, 5 to 6 minutes. Stir in the garlic and cook until fragrant, about 1 minute.

3/ Reduce the heat to medium and add the tomato paste and sun-dried tomatoes, using a spatula to constantly stir and move the tomato paste to prevent it from burning. Cook until the tomato paste has turned a dark brick-red color, about 2 minutes. Add the vegetable stock, soy sauce, balsamic vinegar, lemon juice, mustard, onion powder, garlic powder, and sugar. Stir to combine, then return the mushrooms to the skillet and season with salt and pepper. Bring to a boil over medium-high heat. Reduce the heat to low and simmer until the mixture is slightly thickened and the flavors marry, about 2 minutes. Remove from the heat.

4/ Preheat the oven to broil. Slice the rolls in half lengthwise, cutting only three-quarters of the way through, so the two halves of bread are still attached. Place each roll on an 8 x 12-inch sheet of aluminum foil. Gently cup and crimp the foil around each roll, then divide the mushroom mixture equally among the 4 rolls and top each with 4 slices of cheese.

5/ Broil the sandwiches until the cheese is golden brown and bubbling, 1 to 2 minutes. Remove them from the oven and let cool.

Cola-Braised Brisket Tacos

SERVES 4 TO 6

This dish is inspired by Mexican carnitas ("little meats"), traditionally made by braising pork in fat, often with citrus, spices, and aromatics. I swap the pork for brisket and braise it for hours in a similar mixture, along with cola. I am not a soda person, but Coke really is the secret ingredient to this recipe. It tenderizes the meat, and the sugars from the soda add a rich caramel note. Mexican Coke is ideal for this recipe because it is sweetened with cane sugar instead of the corn syrup that is used in the United States. However, if you can't find Mexican Coke, use regular Coke or even stock with a little brown sugar as a substitute.

COLA-BRAISED BRISKET

2 pounds brisket, trimmed of excess fat, cut in half crosswise

1 tablespoon kosher salt, plus more as needed

½ teaspoon freshly ground black pepper, plus more as needed

2 teaspoons dried oregano

2 teaspoons ground cumin

1 teaspoon chili powder

½ teaspoon ground cinnamon

½ medium yellow onion, cut into wedges

4 large garlic cloves, smashed

Juice of 2 limes

Juice of 1 orange

½ cup Mexican Coca-Cola (see headnote)

1 bay leaf

ASSEMBLY

8 (6-inch) corn tortillas

Pico de Gallo (page 94)

¼ cup fresh cilantro, chopped

1 lime, cut into wedges

1 ripe avocado, peeled, pitted, and sliced

1/ **TO MAKE THE COLA-BRAISED BRISKET ON THE STOVETOP** In a Dutch oven set over medium-high heat, combine the brisket, salt, pepper, oregano, cumin, chili powder, cinnamon, onion, garlic, lime juice, orange juice, cola, and bay leaf. Partially cover it with a lid and bring to a boil, then reduce the heat to low and simmer for 3 to 3½ hours, until the meat is fork-tender, stirring occasionally to prevent sticking. If the liquid drops halfway below the meat, add enough water to just barely cover the brisket and stir to incorporate. When it's done, remove the brisket and place it on a cutting board, reserving the braising liquid. Using two forks, shred the meat into thin strands.

2/ **TO MAKE THE COLA-BRAISED BRISKET IN A SLOW COOKER** In a 6-quart slow cooker, combine the brisket, salt, pepper, oregano, cumin, chili powder, cinnamon, onion, garlic, lime juice, orange juice, cola, and bay leaf. Cover and cook on low for 8 to 10 hours, or on high for 5 to 6 hours, until tender. Remove the brisket and place it on a cutting board, reserving the liquid in the cooker. Using two forks, shred the meat into thin strands.

3/ Preheat the broiler to high and arrange a rack in the upper third of the oven. Lightly spray a sheet pan with cooking oil. Transfer the shredded beef onto the sheet pan and pour 1 cup of the reserved cooking liquid over the meat. Broil until the meat becomes browned and crispy on the edges, 5 to 10 minutes.

4/ Season to taste with salt and pepper. Just before serving, pour more of the cooking liquid over the meat for added flavor.

5/ Carefully char the tortillas over an open flame on a gas grill or stovetop until charred around the edges. (Alternatively, if you don't have a gas grill or stove, preheat the oven to a high broil, place a rack in the upper third, and line a sheet pan with foil. Warm the tortillas under the broiler until slightly charred, 2 to 4 minutes.)

6/ **TO ASSEMBLE** Spoon a few tablespoons of the brisket into the middle of each tortilla. Top with pico de gallo, cilantro, a squeeze of lime juice, and sliced avocado. Serve immediately.

Sweet & Smoky Guac Burger

● **MAKES 4 BURGERS**

I'm just gonna say it: Guacamole is the best topping for a burger, and that's a battle I am prepared to fight! Its creaminess and fattiness pairs perfectly with ground beef, and the better the guacamole, the better your burger will be. Now, the thing that makes this particular guacamole exceptional is that there's not one, not two, but *three* types of citrus mixed in. Lime, lemon, and orange, both juice and zest, add the most balanced combination of sharp acidity and tangy sweetness. Along with the guacamole, I serve my burger with a spicy chipotle ketchup. Fair warning: You'll want to dip absolutely everything into it after you've tasted it, so proceed with caution. This beachy burger hits every single flavor on your palate, and just one bite will transport you to summer days on the Pacific at any time of year.

THREE-CITRUS GUACAMOLE

2 ripe avocados

Zest and juice of 1 lime

1 teaspoon orange zest, plus 1 tablespoon juice

1 teaspoon lemon zest, plus 2 teaspoons juice

½ small red onion, diced (about ⅓ cup)

½ jalapeño, seeded and minced

3 garlic cloves, grated

¼ cup fresh cilantro, chopped

½ teaspoon kosher salt

CHIPOTLE KETCHUP

½ cup ketchup

2 tablespoons mayonnaise

1 canned chipotle pepper in adobo, minced, plus 1 teaspoon adobo sauce

BURGERS

1⅓ pounds (80/20) ground beef

1 teaspoon chipotle powder

½ teaspoon granulated garlic

½ teaspoon ground cumin

Kosher salt and freshly ground black pepper

ASSEMBLY

4 pineapple rings, canned or fresh

4 brioche buns, halved and toasted

4 lettuce leaves

1/ **MAKE THE GUACAMOLE** In a medium bowl, mash the flesh of both avocados using a fork or whisk until mostly smooth. Add the remaining ingredients and stir to combine. Cover with plastic wrap, pressing it onto the surface of the guacamole, and refrigerate until ready to use.

2/ **MAKE THE KETCHUP** In a small bowl, add the ketchup, mayonnaise, chipotle pepper, and adobo sauce and stir to combine. Cover and refrigerate until ready to use.

3/ **MAKE THE BURGERS** In a large bowl, combine the meat, spices, and salt and pepper to taste and gently mix to blend well. Divide the mixture into 4 patties and set aside.

4/ Preheat a large grill pan or cast-iron skillet over medium-high heat. Season each burger with salt and pepper and grill for 3 minutes per side (less time if you prefer your burgers more rare, or a bit longer if you like them well-done). Transfer the burgers to a plate and set aside.

5/ Add the pineapple rings to the same grill pan and cook until lightly charred, about 2 minutes on each side. Remove from the grill.

6/ To assemble, spread a spoonful of chipotle ketchup on a bottom bun. Add 1 lettuce leaf, 1 burger, 1 grilled pineapple slice, and a few spoonfuls of guacamole, then cover with the top bun. Repeat with the remaining burgers and serve.

If you ask my friends or family, they'd probably tell you that snacking is one of my main personality traits.

There isn't enough room in this book to tell you all the reasons I consider snacks an elite food category, so I'll attempt to do them justice in a couple of paragraphs. Snacks can be anything! Salty, sweet, savory, easy, elaborate, lowbrow, or fancy. The one thing they all must have in common is that they are the kind of food you want to keep . . . snacking on. Hence the name!

What differentiates a snack from a meal? How do we really define a snack? Is it a tiny meal? An amuse-bouche? A small plate? A little nosh? Something best at midnight? The truth is that snacks are all these things and more: the joyful food between meals.

We may have only three main meals a day, but you can have an unlimited number of snacks per day, and in this chapter, you'll find a snack for every moment and mood. Sometimes you want something sweet, salty, and even giftable, like the **Salted Brown Sugar Caramel Popcorn** on page 97. Other times you want a simple crowd-pleaser, like **Guac, Salsa & Chips Bar** on page 90. Then, of course, sometimes you need a fancy snack, maybe before a fancy dinner, and the **Crackers & Schmears, 3 Ways** on page 100 are perfect for those moments. With so much variety in this chapter, I dare you to make one of these snacks and not come back!

SNACKS

Sea Salt Focaccia

WITH SUN-DRIED TOMATO SPREAD

● MAKES 12 LARGE PIECES
OR 24 SNACK-SIZE PIECES

When I first started out in the kitchen, I really only liked *cooking.* I thought baking was tedious and intimidating, because it's often such an exact science, whereas cooking leaves much more room for improvisation and experimentation, which always seemed more fun to me. Then one night, I was out to dinner with my family and tried focaccia for the first time; it was so insanely good that I decided learning how to make it at home would be worth the extra effort. After researching different recipes, I learned that it's made from a pretty forgiving dough—even better for my first baking project.

Focaccia is a high-hydration dough, meaning you should get ready for a wet, loose dough while you're kneading. But don't let that scare you; it's really hard to mess this one up! That's thanks to a couple of things, like the long, slow rise, which gives it both that delicious, yeasted flavor and the bubbles that create focaccia's signature tender-and-airy texture. It also has lots and lots of olive oil in it, so make sure you use a high-quality one. Your future self will thank you.

SEA SALT FOCACCIA
1½ cups (355g) warm water (105°F to 110°F)

1 teaspoon sugar

1 (0.25-ounce) packet active dry yeast

3½ cups (490g) bread flour, plus more as needed

¼ cup (40g) semolina flour

1½ teaspoons kosher salt

¼ cup (54g) extra-virgin olive oil, plus more for kneading and drizzling

Flaky sea salt, for sprinkling

1/ **MAKE THE FOCACCIA** In the bowl of a stand mixer fitted with the dough hook attachment, combine the warm water, sugar, and yeast using a fork. Let sit until foamy, about 5 minutes.

2/ In a medium bowl, combine the bread flour, semolina flour, and kosher salt. Carefully add the flour mixture to the stand mixer bowl and mix at a low speed until the dough has become a shaggy mass. Add the olive oil and mix on medium speed until the dough forms a ball, 3 to 5 minutes. If the dough hasn't formed a ball by this time, add 1 tablespoon bread flour at a time, mixing well between each addition, until the dough pulls away from the sides of the bowl. Transfer the dough to a lightly oiled work surface and lightly oil your hands as well.

3/ Knead the dough for 10 minutes, using the slap and fold technique. Working quickly, use both hands to grab the dough in the middle and lift it completely off the work surface, about 8 to 10 inches in the air. The dough will immediately fold in half on itself. Quickly swing the dough away from your body and slap it back down onto the work surface. The dough will be very sticky and wet, so if you struggle to knead it, periodically coat your hands with olive oil, or use a bench scraper to gather any stuck dough from the work surface, and continue kneading.

4/ Once the dough has become more elastic and stretches easily, transfer it to a well-oiled bowl, cover tightly with plastic wrap, and set aside to rise for 1 hour, or until doubled in size.

5/ After the dough has risen, transfer it to an oiled 9 × 13-inch pan and spread it out with your hands. Drizzle more olive oil over the top, then cover and place in the refrigerator to rise for 8 to 12 hours, or overnight.

6/ When ready to bake, remove the pan from the refrigerator and allow the dough to come to room temperature. Meanwhile, preheat the oven to 425°F.

7/ Drizzle more olive oil on the dough and poke it all over, creating dimples covering the surface of the dough. Sprinkle with flaky sea salt and bake the focaccia for 25 to 30 minutes, rotating it halfway through, until golden brown on top. Allow to cool for 15 to 20 minutes before cutting.

8/ Serve the bread warm with the sun-dried tomato spread on the side. (Leftover spread will keep in an airtight container in the refrigerator for up to 3 months.)

Sun-Dried Tomato Spread

Focaccia is great simply dipped in even more olive oil, but if you want to go all the way, this tangy, fruity, sun-dried tomato spread is it. Any leftover spread makes a great addition to a sandwich or a charcuterie or cheese board, or as one of the toppings for the crackers on page 100!

1 (10-ounce) jar sun-dried tomatoes with Italian herbs, packed in oil

1 cup fresh basil leaves

1½ teaspoons packed light brown sugar

2 garlic cloves

½ teaspoon kosher salt, plus more as needed

½ teaspoon sherry vinegar

Combine all the ingredients in the bowl of a food processor or blender. Pulse until combined and season to taste with salt.

QUICK BITE

Leftover focaccia makes a GREAT quick pizza crust! Carefully cut it in half lengthwise through the middle to make two thinner layers. Top each layer with sauce, cheese, and anything else you like, and bake at 450°F until the cheese is melted and bubbly.

Beer Bread

WITH WHIPPED HONEY BUTTER

● **MAKES 1 LOAF**

Before you even start reading this recipe, I should inform you that beer bread is going to ruin all other bread for you. If you're still reading, don't say I didn't warn you! I first came across this bread during an internship I had at a steak house in the summer of 2016. Every single table was served a basket of this bread, which filled the kitchen with the most intoxicating smell each time it was taken out of the oven. Once I managed to try it myself, I immediately fell in love. I asked the chef to teach me how to make it, and now I'm ready to pass along that recipe to you. The not-so-secret ingredient that created that incredible aroma is beer! It adds a deep, yeasty flavor that makes this bread absolutely irresistible. I've added a topping of whipped honey butter to my version, because, as we all know, butter makes everything better, particularly when it's slathered on bread that's still warm from the oven. Not only is this bread delicious, it is also ridiculously easy to make.

BEER BREAD

3 tablespoons (41g) unsalted butter, sliced into ¼-inch pieces, plus more for greasing

2½ cups (350g) all-purpose flour, plus more for dusting

¼ cup (50g) packed light brown sugar

1 tablespoon baking powder

1 teaspoon kosher salt

1 (12-ounce) bottle dark beer, at room temperature

WHIPPED HONEY BUTTER

1 stick (110g) salted butter, at room temperature

2 tablespoons honey

Kosher salt

1/ MAKE THE BREAD Preheat the oven to 350°F. Grease a 5 × 9-inch loaf pan with butter, then dust with flour, tapping out any excess flour.

2/ In a large bowl, mix together the flour, brown sugar, baking powder, and salt. Add the beer and mix until thoroughly combined. Scrape the batter into the prepared pan and top with the slices of butter. Bake for 1 hour, or until golden brown on top and moist crumbs cling to a toothpick when inserted into the center. Allow the bread to cool in the pan for 10 minutes, then remove it and place it on a cooling rack. Cool for 5 to 10 minutes before slicing.

3/ MAKE THE HONEY BUTTER In a stand mixer fitted with the paddle attachment, whip the butter on medium-high speed until somewhat paler in color, 30 to 45 seconds. Add the honey and a pinch of salt and whip on medium-high speed again until the butter is light and fluffy, 30 seconds to 1 minute more.

4/ Serve the bread warm with whipped honey butter on the side.

QUICK BITE

While this bread smells like beer (because it literally contains beer), almost all yeast bread smells a bit like beer before it's cooked. What's causing the smell is, in fact, alcohol produced by the yeast in the rising process. Without getting too scientific, the alcohol is produced by the yeast when it encounters sugar. As a reaction to the sugary environment, the yeast produces ethanol gas. Most of the ethanol is cooked out, which is why you don't get drunk off eating bread. "Quick breads," such as this beer bread, don't contain actual yeast. However, you get an even more intense yeasty flavor because—wait for it—beer is made from yeast.

Guac, Salsa & Chips Bar

● **SERVES 4 TO 6**

Arguably the most important part of any get-together is the chips and dips! Of all the chips-and-dips combos out there, in my opinion tortilla chips, guacamole, and salsa bars are FAR superior! I mean, is it even a party without guacamole?! So you know I had to put together the ultimate spread to get you ready for the next time you need to impress (and feed) a crowd. An essential part of making the perfect chip-and-dip bar is having a loaded guacamole, a chunky salsa, and a smooth salsa; the combo of different textures is a game-changer. I like my chunky salsa sweet—in this case, using mango—and the smooth salsa spicy (from roasted jalapeño). Plus, when you have a nice variety of flavors and textures, there's always something for everyone.

Now, for the chip, your favorite store-bought ones will work, of course. That said, making your own freshly fried tortilla chips is 100 percent worth the time and energy! The way I see it, if you're already making home-made salsas, you might as well go all the way.

Freshly Fried Tortilla Chips

Vegetable oil, for frying
8 (8-inch) corn tortillas
Kosher salt

SERVING

Chunky Mango Salsa (recipe follows)

Salsa de Molcajete (recipe follows)

Grilled Pineapple and Poblano Guacamole (recipe follows)

1/ In a large, wide pot, heat 1 inch of oil to 350°F. Line a sheet pan with paper towels and set it nearby.

2/ Meanwhile, cut the tortillas into six chips each by first cutting the tortilla in half, and then cutting each half into three pieces. Working in batches and using a spider or tongs, transfer the cut tortillas to the hot oil and fry until golden brown on each side, for 30 seconds to 1 minute on each side. Transfer to the prepared sheet pan, season with salt immediately after removing them from the oil, and repeat with the remaining tortillas. Allow the chips to cool slightly before serving with the guacamole and salsas on the side. (The chips can be stored in an airtight container at room temperature for up to 2 days before serving.)

MAKES 1½ CUPS

Chunky Mango Salsa

2 ripe mangos, peeled, pitted, and chopped (about 2 cups)
½ cup diced red onion
½ small jalapeño, minced
Juice and zest of 2 limes
¼ cup cilantro, chopped
Kosher salt

Mix all the ingredients together in a small bowl until well blended. Taste and adjust the salt to your liking. Serve with tortilla chips. (This salsa can be stored in an airtight container in the refrigerator for up to 3 days.)

Salsa de Molcajete

4 plum tomatoes

1 medium jalapeño

2 dried chiles de árbol (or any dried red chili)

3 large garlic cloves, unpeeled

Juice of 1 lime

Kosher salt

1/ In a cast-iron skillet set over medium-high heat, roast the tomatoes, jalapeño, chiles de árbol, and garlic, turning occasionally with tongs. When the papery outer skin of the garlic starts to brown, after 6 to 8 minutes, remove the garlic from the pan and carefully peel it, discarding the skin. Continue roasting the tomatoes, jalapeño, and chiles until soft and blackened on all sides, another 8 minutes. Transfer to a plate to cool. Trim the stem off the jalapeño and deseed it, if you desire a milder salsa.

2/ Place the garlic cloves and salt in the bowl of the molcajete and grind with the pestle to a paste. Add the chiles de árbol and continue grinding until they break into small pieces. Add the jalapeño and continue grinding until it is worked into a paste. Add the tomatoes, one at a time, and grind until smooth. (Alternatively, place all the ingredients into the bowl of a food processor or a high-speed blender and purée until smooth.)

3/ Add the lime juice and season the salsa generously with salt to taste. Serve warm or allow it to chill in the refrigerator and serve cold.

QUICK BITE

A molcajete is a type of mortar and pestle used in Mexican cooking. ("Salsa de molcajete" can refer to any salsa made in a molcajete.) Molcajetes are traditionally made of basalt, which gives their surface a rough texture that is ideal for grinding spices, chili peppers, and other ingredients. Grinding ingredients in a molcajete releases more flavors and aromas than chopping them in a food processor does, and it's a lot of fun, so I encourage you to seek one out!

Grilled Pineapple and Poblano Guacamole

½ pineapple, peeled, cored, and cut lengthwise into planks

1 medium poblano pepper

4 ripe avocados

Juice of 1 lime

Juice of ½ lemon

½ small white onion, finely diced

1 large garlic clove, minced

1 tablespoon chopped fresh cilantro

Kosher salt and freshly ground black pepper

¼ cup queso fresco, crumbled (optional)

1/ Preheat a grill to medium-high or set a grill pan over medium-high heat. Grill the pineapple planks until they are charred, about 3 minutes per side. Let cool slightly, then chop them into ½-inch cubes. Set aside.

2/ Place the poblano directly on the grates of a gas stove burner and turn on a high flame underneath it. Using tongs, carefully turn the poblano occasionally to char it on all sides, about 2 minutes per side. (If you don't have gas burners, heat your broiler to high and place a rack in the upper third of your oven. Line a sheet pan with foil and place the poblano on the sheet pan. Rotate the pepper under the broiler until charred on all sides, about 2 minutes per side, but keep an eye on it, because all broilers are different. You can also do this with the pineapple if you don't have a grill or grill pan.)

3/ Once the poblano is charred, place it in a large bowl and cover it with plastic wrap. Allow the poblano to steam until softened, about 10 minutes. Remove the plastic wrap carefully. Once the poblano has cooled slightly, use your hands to peel back the burnt skin. Discard the skin, along with the stem and seeds. Chop the poblano into bite-size pieces and set aside.

4/ In the same bowl, roughly mash the avocado. Add the lime juice, lemon juice, onion, garlic, cilantro, poblano, and pineapple, reserving some for garnish. Season with salt and pepper. Top with reserved pineapple and queso fresco (if using). Serve immediately.

Queso Fundido

SERVES 8

If you've never had queso fundido, think of it as regular queso's sophisticated, older sibling. (Some might say it's the FUN-dido version of queso??) This Tex-Mex classic originated around campfires near the US-Mexico border, but you don't need to wait for a camping trip to give this a try; you can replicate the heat and smoke of a campfire pretty well in your home kitchen, thanks to the spice blend in this recipe.

Now, I have to be bossy about one thing, and that's do NOT use preshredded cheese. It's coated in a powder so that it doesn't melt or stick together during shipping and storing, and that powder coating will be a REAL detriment to the final texture and flavor of this dish. So grate your own cheese, please!

PICO DE GALLO

2 small tomatoes, chopped (about ½ cup)

¼ cup chopped onion

1 teaspoon diced jalapeño

Juice of ½ lime

1 tablespoon chopped fresh oregano

1 tablespoon chopped fresh cilantro

Kosher salt and freshly ground black pepper

QUESO FUNDIDO

1 teaspoon vegetable oil

8 ounces ground protein (I use plant-based) or chorizo (see Quick Bite)

½ teaspoon ground cumin

½ teaspoon sweet paprika

½ teaspoon dried oregano

¼ teaspoon chipotle powder (optional)

¼ teaspoon kosher salt

¼ teaspoon freshly ground black pepper

½ poblano pepper, chopped

⅓ cup diced yellow onion

2 garlic cloves, minced

1 tablespoon all-purpose flour

1 cup light beer, such as Tecate

1 (8-ounce) block yellow cheddar cheese, coarsely grated

1 (8-ounce) block Monterey Jack cheese, coarsely grated

1 tablespoon chopped fresh oregano

1 tablespoon chopped fresh cilantro

8 (8-inch) flour tortillas, warmed, for serving

1/ **MAKE THE PICO DE GALLO** In a bowl, combine all the ingredients, adding salt and pepper to taste.

2/ **MAKE THE QUESO FUNDIDO** Set a large skillet over medium-high heat and add the oil. Once it's hot and shimmering, add the ground protein and cook until lightly browned, 2 to 3 minutes. Add the cumin, paprika, dried oregano, chipotle powder (if using), salt, and black pepper and mix until combined. Cook for 1 minute, then add the poblano and onion and cook until lightly caramelized, 4 to 5 minutes. Add the garlic and cook until fragrant, about 1 minute. Reduce the heat to medium, sprinkle the flour over the top, and stir to combine. Cook until the flour has been absorbed into the mixture, about 2 minutes.

3/ Add the beer and stir thoroughly to combine. Bring to a boil over medium-high heat, then reduce the heat to low. Simmer until the mixture begins to thicken, 2 to 3 minutes. Whisk the cheeses into the pan, a small handful at a time, until completely melted. Transfer to a medium heatproof bowl and top with Pico de Gallo and chopped oregano and cilantro. Serve immediately while hot with warm tortillas on the side.

QUICK BITE

This recipe calls for ground protein and a mix of spices to give this cheese dip its kick, but if you can find fresh chorizo or a plant-based version, you could substitute that for the "meat" and spices. Just omit the cumin, paprika, dried oregano, and chipotle powder.

Salted Brown Sugar Caramel Popcorn

● MAKES 6 CUPS

Someone has to say it, so it's gonna be me: People treat caramel popcorn as a seasonal snack and it shouldn't be! Free caramel popcorn from the holiday season! Caramel popcorn is something most people buy and have never made at home, but the homemade version is infinitely better. Plus, I can almost guarantee you that you really do always have the ingredients for it in your pantry. I know that caramel can be intimidating, but I developed and tested this method a TON to make sure it's both easy *and* foolproof, and it really is! After 4 short minutes on the stovetop, the oven does the rest of the work to cook the caramel to a perfect, crunchy final texture. I like mine with extra flaky salt at the end to balance the sweetness, and the caramel keeps the popcorn fresh for days. It's the perfect snack to keep or share—or better yet, both!

Nonstick cooking spray

6 cups popped popcorn (about 3 tablespoons of kernels), either popped on the stovetop or in the microwave

½ stick salted butter

1 cup firmly packed dark brown sugar

¼ cup light corn syrup

1 teaspoon kosher salt

1 teaspoon pure vanilla extract

¼ teaspoon baking soda

Flaky sea salt, for sprinkling

1/ Preheat the oven to 250°F. Line a large sheet pan with parchment paper. Coat a large ovenproof bowl with nonstick spray and put the popcorn in it. Place the popcorn in the oven as it preheats; warming the popcorn will help the caramel coat it more evenly.

2/ In a 12-inch nonstick skillet set over medium heat, melt the butter, then whisk in the brown sugar, corn syrup, and kosher salt. Bring to a boil, whisking constantly. Once the mixture boils, cook without stirring for 4 minutes. Remove from the heat and whisk in the vanilla and baking soda; the mixture should bubble up, aerate, and lighten in color (thanks to the baking soda). Remove the warmed popcorn from the oven and immediately pour the caramel over it in a thin stream, stirring with a nonstick spatula to coat the popcorn evenly and thoroughly.

3/ Transfer the popcorn to the prepared sheet pan, spreading it out in an even layer, then place it in the oven for 45 minutes, stirring every 15 minutes to ensure an even coating of caramel. Remove from the oven and top with flaky salt. Allow to cool and harden, then enjoy! (Leftover caramel can be stored in resealable plastic bags or an airtight container, and will keep for 1 week.)

QUICK BITE

Forty-five minutes in the oven may seem odd at first, but the slow-and-low bake lets the brown sugar caramelize gently and takes out the guesswork of making caramel entirely on the stovetop. This also helps you achieve the perfect coverage on each kernel, because it keeps the caramel from setting before it fully coats the popcorn. This recipe makes a very thoroughly coated caramel corn, so add more popcorn at the beginning if you like yours a little less sweet!

Classic Soft Pretzels

● MAKES 8 PRETZELS

Whether dipped in mustard, cheese sauce, or coated in cinnamon sugar, there is nothing like a freshly baked soft pretzel to make any carb lover go a little crazy. When I was a kid, we always used to have frozen pretzels that I'd warm up for an after-school snack. I have re-created that treat I loved so much but in a home-made and—if I may say so myself—vastly improved version of that nostalgic food. The secret to great pretzels is in the baking-soda boiling process, which creates a chemical reaction that results in that dark brown, flavorful crust that everyone loves. This recipe will give you classic soft-yet-chewy pretzels, perfect for sweet or savory dips and toppings, but also great on their own!

1½ cups (365g) whole milk

3 tablespoons dark brown sugar

1 (0.25-ounce) packet active dry yeast

4½ cups (630g) all-purpose flour

½ stick (55g) unsalted butter, melted

2 teaspoons kosher salt

Vegetable oil, for greasing

¾ cup (216g) baking soda

1 large egg, lightly beaten

Pretzel salt or flaky sea salt, for sprinkling

Spicy brown mustard, for serving

1/ In a small saucepan, heat the milk over low heat until warm to the touch. (If you have a thermometer it should be about 105°F, but no warmer than 110°F.) In the bowl of a stand mixer fitted with the dough hook attachment, combine the warm milk and the brown sugar and mix until the sugar dissolves, then sprinkle the yeast on top. Set aside for 5 minutes, or until the mixture begins to foam. Add the flour, butter, and kosher salt to the bowl. Mix on low speed until well combined, then increase the speed to medium and mix until the dough is smooth and pulls away from the sides of the bowl, 4 to 5 minutes.

2/ Remove the bowl from the stand mixer and drizzle a few tablespoons of oil over top of the dough. Toss the dough ball in the oil, then cover with plastic wrap, and let sit in a warm place for approximately 1 hour, or until the dough has doubled in size.

3/ Preheat the oven to 450°F. Line two sheet pans with parchment paper and set aside.

4/ In a large pot over medium heat, add 10 cups water and the baking soda and bring to a very light boil. Turn the dough out onto a lightly oiled work surface and divide it into 8 equal-size pieces. Roll each piece into a 24-inch rope, keeping the ends narrow and the center slightly thicker. Make a U shape with the rope and cross the ends over

each other leaving a ½-inch to 1-inch space between them. Press the tips onto the bottom of the U to shape the pretzel.

5/ Using clean hands or a large flat spatula, place the pretzels in the boiling water, one at a time. Cook for 30 seconds on each side, then remove them from the water with the spatula and place on the prepared sheet pans, brush the top of each pretzel with the beaten egg, and sprinkle pretzel salt over them. Bake until dark golden brown, 10 to 15 minutes.

6/ Transfer to a cooling rack for at least 5 minutes. Serve with spicy brown mustard. (The pretzels are best eaten within a day, though they can be frozen for up to a month.)

QUICK BITE

If you have never made pretzels before, you might be confused by the step of boiling the dough briefly in a mixture of baking soda and water. It may sound like a useless step that you can skip, but it's actually what makes pretzels, pretzels! Dropping each pretzel in the boiling mixture causes the interior of the pretzel to puff up and begins the crust formation. The baking soda makes the water very alkaline, which gives the pretzels their brown, shiny crust and their distinctive flavor.

Crackers & Schmears, 3 Ways

The beginnings of this snack were inspired by my Grandpa Larry, who was the biggest fan of lox and cream cheese. He definitely bought his lox, but making your own is a great project to try at home. This method will teach you the basics of curing, and working with lox is much easier than other meats. The curing process transforms the fish's texture and flavor, and the beets give it a beautiful pink-to-purple ombré color. The assembly couldn't be simpler, and the colors couldn't be more beautiful!

You know I can't give you just one cracker topping combo, so here are a couple other favorites: I make the fig and goat cheese crackers when I am feeling bougie or need to impress some hungry friends but am short on time. The sweet, salt, and tang of this combination is no-brainer delicious, and the figs make this combo feel extra fancy. What I'm trying to say is, if this cracker were a person, it would wear a monocle.

Another favorite is a Mediterranean-inspired cracker, which you should definitely try no matter what, but especially if you've made my Sun-Dried Tomato Spread (page 85), because you'll already have half the ingredients! This one is topped with some of the spread and a delicious lemony whipped feta. Like the other variations, this combination sounds elaborate, but in this case, the food processer does all the work.

You can certainly get away with making these one at a time, but if you're having some people over and you know they'll get hungry (who doesn't?), why not be a cracker triple threat and make them all?

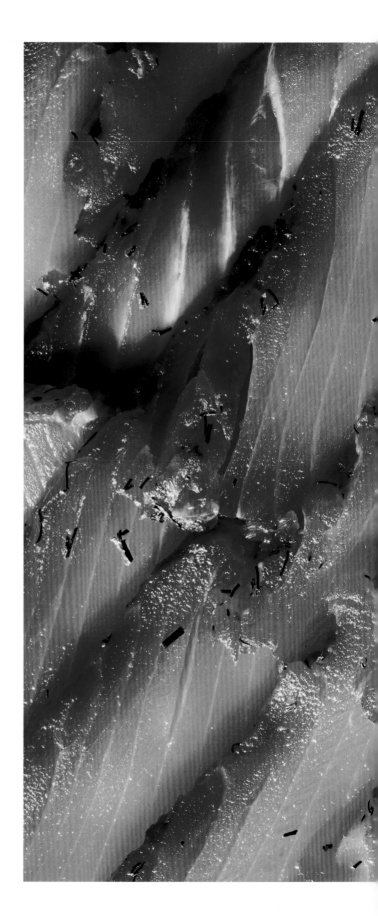

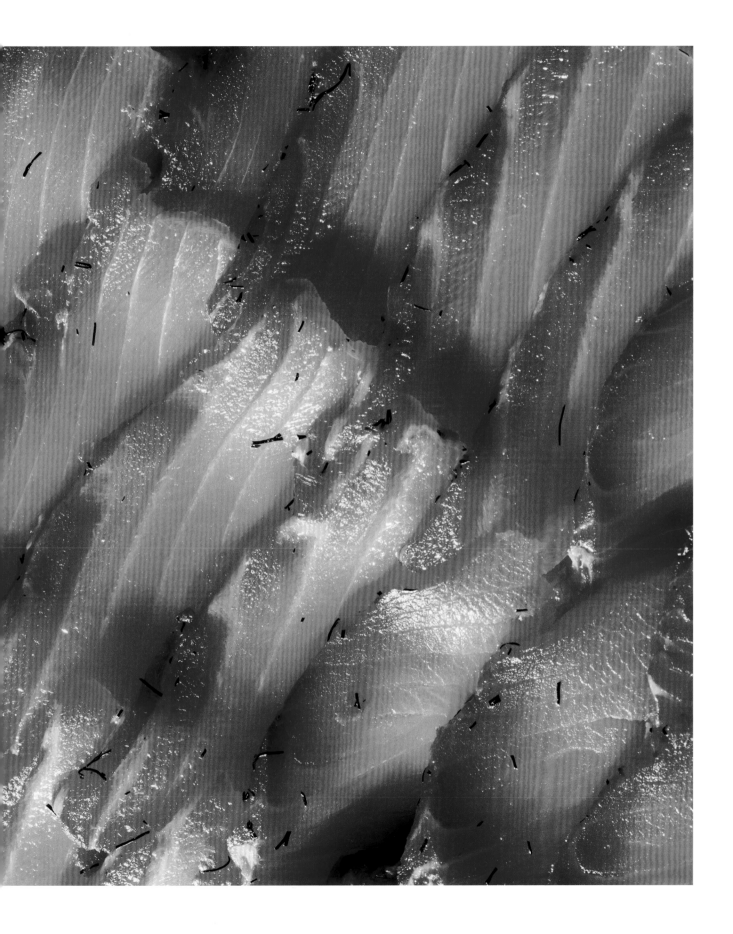

Crackers with Scallion Cream Cheese and Beet-Cured Salmon

1 (8-ounce) block cream cheese

3 scallions, green and white parts, trimmed and cut into thirds

½ teaspoon kosher salt

Freshly ground black pepper

1 (8.5-ounce) box Triscuits or other crackers of your choice

1 pound Beet-Cured Salmon (recipe follows) or store-bought lox, thinly sliced into ribbons

Fresh dill, for garnish

1/ In the bowl of a food processor, combine the cream cheese, scallions, salt, and pepper to taste. Process until the scallions are finely chopped and evenly distributed.

2/ Arrange the crackers on a serving platter. Spread each cracker with about 2 teaspoons of the cream cheese mixture and top with a ribbon of beet-cured salmon. Garnish with fresh dill and serve immediately.

Beet-Cured Salmon

2 small beets, peeled and finely grated (about 1 cup)

¼ cup roughly chopped fresh dill

3 tablespoons kosher salt

1½ tablespoons sugar

Freshly ground black pepper

1 pound skin-on center-cut salmon

1/ In a large bowl, mix together the beets, dill, salt, sugar, and pepper to taste. Place the salmon on a piece of parchment paper and apply the mixture all over the flesh side, packing it gently onto the surface.

2/ Wrap the salmon tightly in the parchment paper and place it on a large plate. Set a smaller plate on top and weight it down, using two heavy cans or something similar. Place it in the refrigerator and let cure until the flesh is firm to the touch, 3 to 4 days. On the second day, flip the salmon over, top again with the smaller plate, and replace the weights.

3/ Once the salmon has cured, wipe off the beet-dill mixture and discard. Thinly slice the salmon against the grain, using a thin, long knife. (The sliced salmon will keep, refrigerated in an airtight container, for about 1 week.)

Crackers with Whipped Feta and Sun-Dried Tomato Spread

1 (6-ounce) block feta cheese

3 ounces cream cheese (about ⅓ cup), at room temperature

2 tablespoons extra-virgin olive oil

Zest and juice of ½ lemon

Kosher salt and freshly ground black pepper

1 (8.5-ounce) box Ritz crackers or other crackers of your choice

½ cup Sun-Dried Tomato Spread (page 85)

1/ In the bowl of a food processor, combine the feta, cream cheese, and olive oil and process until light and airy, about 2 minutes. Add the lemon zest and juice, pulse the food processor a few times, then taste and season with salt and pepper.

2/ Arrange the crackers on a sheet pan or serving platter. Spread each with about 2 teaspoons of the whipped feta, then top with sun-dried tomato spread and pepper. Serve immediately.

Crackers with Goat Cheese, Fig, and Balsamic Reduction

¼ cup balsamic vinegar

1 tablespoon light brown sugar

12 figs, fresh or dried

1 (8.5-ounce) box water crackers or crackers of your choice

1 (6-ounce) log goat cheese, softened

Freshly ground black pepper and flaky sea salt, for sprinkling

1/ In a small saucepot set over medium-high heat, combine the vinegar and brown sugar. Bring the mixture to a boil, then reduce the heat to low and cook for 15 minutes, or until the mixture has thickened and reduced by three-quarters. Remove from the heat and set aside to cool.

2/ While the reduction is cooking, halve or quarter the figs, depending on their size. Set aside.

3/ Arrange the crackers on a sheet pan or serving platter. Spread each cracker with about 2 teaspoons of the goat cheese, then top with a few fig pieces. Drizzle the crackers with the balsamic reduction and sprinkle with pepper and flaky salt. Serve immediately.

Buffalo Cauliflower Bites

WITH RANCH DIPPING SAUCE

● **SERVES 4**

Right after potatoes, cauliflower takes a very solid second place in my personal vegetable ranking. It's taken this spot somewhat recently, and that's because I love that it has a texture that's both vegetal AND hearty. Of course, I don't need to tell you that spicy buffalo sauce and cool, creamy ranch are a classic combination, but I *will* tell you that the chickpea flour is a game-changer here. I've been served my fair share of baked vegetables that were supposed to be crispy but just weren't, and my chickpea batter solves this problem. It creates an airy-but-still-crunchy texture that stands up to the buffalo sauce coating and any amount of ranch you choose to dip into. These make an incredible alternative to chicken wings for game day—especially if you find yourself with a head of cauliflower languishing in your vegetable drawer—and they're just as satisfying, too!

BUFFALO CAULIFLOWER

1 cup chickpea flour

1 teaspoon kosher salt

1 teaspoon smoked paprika

½ teaspoon garlic powder

¼ teaspoon cayenne pepper

Freshly ground black pepper

2 small heads of cauliflower, cut into florets (about 6 cups)

2 tablespoons unsalted butter, melted

½ cup cayenne pepper hot sauce (I like Frank's RedHot)

1 tablespoon honey

RANCH DIPPING SAUCE

½ cup sour cream

¼ cup mayonnaise

2 tablespoons milk

Zest of ½ lemon

2 teaspoons lemon juice

1 tablespoon Dijon mustard

1 garlic clove, finely minced or grated

2 tablespoons minced fresh chives

2 tablespoons minced fresh dill

2 tablespoons minced fresh parsley

Kosher salt and freshly ground black pepper

1/ Preheat the oven to 450°F and line two rimmed sheet pans with parchment paper.

2/ **PREPARE THE CAULIFLOWER** In a large bowl, combine the chickpea flour and 1 cup cold water and whisk until smooth. Add the salt, smoked paprika, garlic powder, cayenne, and black pepper to taste and mix until combined. Add the cauliflower florets and toss until they are evenly coated. Divide the cauliflower between the prepared sheet pans. Place in the oven and bake for 30 minutes, or until crisp and golden brown, tossing the florets and rotating the pans halfway through.

3/ While the cauliflower bakes, combine the melted butter, hot sauce, and honey in a large bowl and whisk until emulsified. Set aside at room temperature.

4/ Once the cauliflower has baked for 30 minutes, remove it from the oven and let cool slightly. Add it to the bowl with the butter mixture and toss to evenly coat. Divide the cauliflower between the prepared sheet pans and return them to the oven for 10 minutes. Flip the cauliflower and bake for an additional 10 minutes, or until very crisp.

5/ **MAKE THE RANCH SAUCE** Combine all the ingredients in a medium bowl, adding salt and black pepper to taste, and whisk until well blended. Cover and store in the refrigerator until ready to serve.

6/ Remove the cauliflower from the oven and place it on a large serving platter with the ranch dipping sauce on the side.

Not-Your-Bubbe's Onion Dip

● SERVES 6 (MAKES ABOUT 2 CUPS)

I love French onion dip, so in classic Eitan fashion, I wanted to figure out how to make the best version ever. And you know what makes onion dip better? Adding not one, not two, but THREE members of the allium family! My dip has leeks for gentle earthy flavor, shallots for depth and sweetness, and fresh scallions on top for a sharp onion flavor that balances the creamy dip beautifully.

But wait! We're not done with the onion improvements. I could not resist adding in my absolute favorite allium-cooking technique: caramelizing! (True story: Once, at a restaurant with my family, I ordered a side of caramelized onions because I love them that much. Rather than a small plate, the waiter brought me an entire platter of caramelized onions, and I couldn't have been happier!) This dip is my tribute to the great technique of caramelization, and I'm confident it does one of my very favorite foods justice.

¼ cup olive oil

4 cups thinly sliced cleaned leeks, pale green and white parts only (about 2 small bunches)

6 medium shallots, thinly sliced

Kosher salt and freshly ground black pepper

½ cup sour cream

¼ cup mayonnaise

½ teaspoon garlic powder

Juice of ½ lemon

3 scallions, green part, thinly sliced on the bias

Crackers and mixed crudités, such as carrots, peppers, and celery, for serving

1/ In a 12-inch skillet set over medium heat, add the oil, followed by the leeks and shallots. Season with salt and pepper and stir to combine. Allow the mixture to sweat, stirring every few minutes and being sure to gently scrape the bottom of the pan to incorporate any browned bits. If the mixture begins to stick to the bottom of the pan, pour in ¼ cup water and use a spatula to loosen the mixture. Repeat this as needed and cook until it is jammy and golden brown, 40 to 45 minutes. Transfer to a large heatproof bowl and cool to room temperature.

2/ Once cooled, add the sour cream, mayonnaise, garlic powder, and lemon juice and stir to combine. Taste and season with salt and pepper. Refrigerate until fully chilled, 20 to 30 minutes, then top with the scallions and serve with crackers and crudités. (Leftover dip will keep in the refrigerator, covered, for about 3 days.)

Chaat

WITH ALL THE CHUTNEYS

● SERVES 4 TO 6

An essential component of any Indian meal is the many little bowls of chutneys and raitas that come with it. The simplest description of chutney is that it's a sauce or condiment, but there's a whole lot more going on than what's in the bottles that line refrigerator shelves. Most chutneys are a blend of fruits and/or vegetables with other (often savory or tangy) ingredients, such as vinegars, oils, herbs, and spices, mixed in. Chutneys can be used on their own to enhance the flavor profile of breads, curries, and meat dishes, but they can be layered together to create an even more deliciously complex depth of flavor. Raitas are yogurt-and-herb-based sauces, often containing chopped vegetables, like cucumber or eggplant, that add a cooling note to an otherwise spicy meal.

Chutneys are made all over India in countless regional variations, but here, I'm sharing my three staple chutneys, which are also three of the most traditional, as they are produced in many states across the Indian subcontinent. These chutneys have very different flavors from one another, so they give you all the tools for a deliciously balanced Indian meal: The tamarind chutney tastes sweet, sour, and tangy all at once; the mint chutney is smooth and fresh but surprisingly spicy; and the mango chutney is sweet, fruity, and juicy. Whether you eat them individually or layer them all together as accompaniments to your favorite Indian dish or breads, chutneys and raitas will open your eyes to the ways these special condiments maximize the flavor of anything they're served with. For a snack or an appetizer, try them on top of this papdi chaat for an at-home version of a traditional Indian street food.

Papdi Chaat

2 cups whole wheat flour, preferably atta or finely ground whole wheat flour (see Quick Bite, page 67)

¼ teaspoon kosher salt

2 tablespoons vegetable oil, plus more for frying

ASSEMBLY

Tamarind Chutney (recipe follows)

Mint Chutney (recipe follows)

Mango Chutney (recipe follows)

Cucumber Raita (recipe follows)

Chopped red onion, fresh cilantro leaves, and puffed rice, for garnish

1/ In a large bowl, mix the flour, salt, and vegetable oil to combine. Add ⅔ cup water and, using your hands, mix until a ball of dough forms. Knead on a clean surface until it comes together into a smooth ball and no longer sticks to your hands and work surface. Cover with plastic wrap and let the dough rest for at least 30 minutes or up to 1 hour.

2/ In a medium deep skillet over medium heat, add vegetable oil to a depth of 1 inch and heat to 375°F.

3/ Divide the dough into four pieces and roll them out, one at a time, to a ⅛-inch thickness. Using a 2-inch cookie cutter, cut each piece into 15 to 17 disks. Poke both sides of the disks all over with a fork.

4/ Working in batches and using a spider strainer, lower 6 to 8 disks into the oil, being careful not to overcrowd the pan, and fry until golden brown on both sides, about 30 seconds per side. Transfer the fried dough to a wire rack to cool completely. Repeat with the remaining batches of dough.

5/ Right before serving, lay out a handful of papdi on a platter. Top each cracker with a drizzle of each chutney and the raita, then garnish with chopped onion, cilantro leaves, and puffed rice. Serve immediately, laying out more papdi as needed.

MAKES 1½ CUPS

Tamarind Chutney

1 (14-ounce) packet wet tamarind

2 teaspoons vegetable oil

½ teaspoon cumin seeds

1 teaspoon grated fresh ginger

1 teaspoon grated garlic

1 teaspoon kosher salt

1 whole Kashmiri chili pepper or ½ teaspoon chili powder

1½ cups packed dark brown sugar

1/ In a medium pot, combine 2 cups water and the tamarind. Bring to a boil over high heat, then reduce the heat to low and simmer until the pulp has separated from the seeds and is fully dissolved, stirring occasionally, about 30 minutes. Set a fine-mesh strainer over a medium bowl and pour in the tamarind, using the back of a wooden spoon to push the pulp through.

2/ In a medium pot, heat the oil over medium-high. Add the cumin seeds and stir until aromatic, about 1 minute. Add the ginger and garlic and stir continuously for 1 minute. Pour in the strained pulp, salt, chili, brown sugar, and ¾ cup water. Mix until combined, then bring to a simmer. Reduce the heat to low and simmer until the chutney has a consistency of thin jam, 30 to 40 minutes. Discard the chili (if used). Let cool before serving. (The chutney will keep in the refrigerator for up to 3 weeks.)

MAKES 1 CUP

Mint Chutney

1½ cups packed fresh mint leaves

1 cup packed fresh cilantro leaves

1 green chile, chopped (optional)

1 (½-inch) piece fresh ginger, peeled and roughly chopped

2 garlic cloves

Juice of 1 lemon

½ teaspoon ground cumin

½ teaspoon garam masala (optional)

½ teaspoon kosher salt

In the bowl of a food processor or blender, pulse all the ingredients with ¼ cup water into a rough purée. If more water is needed to achieve a pourable consistency, add 1 tablespoon at a time. Transfer to a resealable airtight jar. (The chutney will keep in the refrigerator for up to 4 days.)

Mango Chutney

5 ripe but firm mangos, peeled and cut into 1-inch cubes

1 (2-inch) cinnamon stick

4 whole cloves

1 teaspoon cumin seeds

1 teaspoon coriander seeds

6 green cardamom pods, cracked with the side of a knife or in a mortar and pestle

1 teaspoon grated fresh ginger

1 garlic clove, crushed with the side of a knife

½ cup white vinegar

1 whole dried red chile (optional)

1 teaspoon kosher salt

2 cups packed light brown sugar, or to taste

1/ In a large saucepan, combine the mangos, cinnamon, cloves, cumin, coriander, cardamom, ginger, garlic, and 2 cups water. Bring to a boil over high heat, then reduce the heat to low and simmer until the mixture has reduced and slightly thickened, about 10 minutes.

2/ Add the vinegar, chile (if using), salt, and brown sugar. Bring to a boil over high heat, then reduce the heat to low and simmer until it is a jam consistency, 30 to 40 minutes. Discard the cinnamon stick, cardamom, chile (if used), and cloves. Let cool before serving. (The chutney will keep in the refrigerator for up to 4 weeks.)

Cucumber Raita

½ cup plain full-fat yogurt

1 small Persian cucumber, grated on the large holes of a box grater

2 tablespoons finely chopped red onion

1 tablespoon chopped fresh cilantro

1 teaspoon lemon zest

1 tablespoon lemon juice

¼ teaspoon grated fresh ginger

Kosher salt

1 teaspoon vegetable oil

6 to 8 curry leaves (optional)

1 teaspoon cumin seeds

1 teaspoon black mustard seeds

1/ In a medium bowl, combine the yogurt, cucumber, red onion, cilantro, lemon zest and juice, and ginger. Taste and season with salt.

2/ In a small frying pan, heat the oil over medium-high heat. Add the curry leaves (if using), cumin seeds, and black mustard seeds. Fry for 30 seconds, or until the cumin seeds begin to pop. Immediately pour the fried spices on top of the raita and slightly mix them in. Transfer to a resealable airtight container and let cool. (The raita will keep in the refrigerator for up to 3 days.)

Tahini Dark Chocolate Puppy Chow

● **MAKES ABOUT 12 CUPS**

I'm pretty certain puppy chow (aka Muddy Buddies) is the most addictive sweet snack in the world. They have all the qualities that make prepackaged foods so good: the perfect balance of fat, sweetness, salt, and a slight bitterness from the dark chocolate. Those kinds of store-bought snacks have entire teams of food scientists that craft the perfect, cravable flavor that keeps you coming back for more and more; this recipe achieves that same near-scientific perfected balance, made easily in your home kitchen.

The key to taking this treat to the next level is freezing the mixture and serving it super cold. This makes the texture of the chocolate and tahini even crunchier, but more importantly, it changes the flavor profile, too. When the chocolate starts out cold instead of at room temperature, you taste the confectioners' sugar immediately, but then the chocolate blooms and the nuttiness of the tahini isn't far behind. Once you try them frozen, you won't want them any other way!

This recipe was the first one I ever developed, so it's not only super easy but it also holds a special place in my heart. If you want to try an easy recipe from my book, this is the one!

1½ cups dark chocolate chips
1 cup well-stirred tahini
2 tablespoons unsalted butter

1 teaspoon pure vanilla extract
Pinch of kosher salt
1 (12-ounce) box Rice Chex cereal

1½ cups confectioners' sugar, sifted
2 tablespoons toasted sesame seeds

1 / Set up a double boiler by bringing a few inches of water to a simmer in a small saucepan, then place a heatproof metal or glass bowl directly on top of the saucepan. (Make sure the water is not touching the bottom of the bowl.) Add the chocolate chips to the bowl and stir until fully melted. Add the tahini, butter, vanilla, and salt, then stir until fully combined and melted. Remove from the heat. (Alternatively, in a microwave-safe bowl, microwave the chocolate on high in 30-second intervals, stirring after each, until fully melted, then add the remaining ingredients and stir until well combined.)

2 / Pour the cereal into a large bowl, then pour the melted chocolate mixture over the cereal. Mix until fully combined. Pour half of the confectioners' sugar over the cereal and stir until combined. Add the remaining confectioners' sugar and sesame seeds to the bowl and mix again until every piece is fully coated.

3 / Line a sheet pan with parchment paper. Transfer the mixture to the prepared sheet pan, spreading it in an even layer. Place in the freezer and chill for at least 30 minutes, until the chocolate solidifies. Serve cold. (Leftovers will keep in a resealable bag in the freezer for up to a month.)

Throughout my life, I've had a . . . let's say, *complex* relationship with vegetables. As a child, I absolutely, point-blank refused to eat them (sorry, Mom and Dad!), preferring to sustain myself on chocolate chip cookies and cinnamon buns. I may have been missing essential vitamins and nutrients, but my childhood taste buds couldn't have been happier!

Luckily, as I got older and began cooking more, my eyes were opened. I realized that I didn't dislike vegetables as a food group, but I DID dislike how they'd been cooked when I had tried them before. The recipes in this chapter are geared toward all the other little Eitans out there who are positive they hate vegetables but probably just haven't had them prepared in a truly delicious way. Whether you identify as a little Eitan or not, these recipes will be your gateway into veggie heaven! I've actually caught myself craving the Brussels sprouts regularly (please don't tell my parents that, though).

VEGGIES

Tahini Caesar

WITH CRISPY PARMESAN & FRIED CAPERS

● SERVES 4

This is a Middle Eastern spin on one of the greatest and most beloved salads of all time: the Caesar! Although Caesar salad is associated with Italian cooking (it was invented by an Italian chef named Caesar Cardini in the 1920s, though he was actually in Mexico at the time), with a couple of tweaks its flavor profile can deliciously shift toward the Middle East. A traditional Caesar gets its mouthwatering umami quality from Parmesan cheese and anchovies, which is cut by a creamy, egg-based dressing. This version kicks up the Parmesan factor by crisping the cheese in the oven so that it has a satisfying crunch, and swaps the anchovy and egg for capers and tahini. Finally, it wouldn't be Caesar without great croutons, and these are made in a way that both Italy and the Middle East would agree on: fried in olive oil.

CRISPY PARMESAN

1½ cups shredded Parmesan cheese

1 tablespoon all-purpose flour

Freshly ground black pepper

DRESSING

¼ cup well-stirred tahini

¼ cup olive oil

Zest and juice from ½ large lemon

1 tablespoon Dijon mustard

1 garlic clove, minced

1 teaspoon reduced-sodium soy sauce or tamari

Kosher salt and freshly ground black pepper

SALAD

3 tablespoons olive oil

2 cups torn (1-inch pieces) crusty bread, preferably sourdough

Kosher salt and freshly ground black pepper

2 tablespoons drained capers, patted dry with paper towels

2 heads romaine lettuce, cored and chopped

1/ **MAKE THE CRISPY PARMESAN** Preheat the oven to 375°F and line a sheet pan with parchment paper.

2/ Combine the cheese, flour, and pepper to taste in a medium bowl. Mound tablespoon portions of the cheese mixture on the prepared sheet pan, leaving about 3 inches between them. Using the back of a spoon, spread each mound into a 3-inch round. Bake until crisp and golden brown, about 10 minutes. Gently transfer to a plate to cool and repeat with the remaining cheese mixture.

3/ **MAKE THE DRESSING** Whisk all the ingredients together in a small bowl, adding salt and pepper to taste. Slowly stream in 2 tablespoons cold water and whisk to combine. The dressing should have a thin, pourable consistency. (If the dressing is too thick, add additional water, 1 tablespoon at a time.) Set aside.

4/ **MAKE THE SALAD** To make the croutons, heat 2 tablespoons of the olive oil in a large skillet over medium heat. Once hot and shimmering, add the bread pieces, tossing to coat them in the oil, and cook until golden brown and crisp on all sides, about 5 minutes.

5/ Remove the croutons from the pan, sprinkle with salt and pepper to taste, and set aside on a plate. In the same skillet, heat the remaining tablespoon olive oil. Once hot and shimmering, add the capers and cook until they "pop" and begin to crisp on the outside, 1 to 2 minutes. Using a slotted spoon, remove them from the oil and let drain on a paper towel–lined plate.

6/ Divide the chopped romaine among four salad plates. Top with the croutons, fried capers, and crispy Parmesan, then drizzle with the tahini dressing.

Smashed Cucumber Salad

● SERVES 4

When the thought of eating something hot and heavy is the last thing in the world you want to do, might I suggest that you try this recipe? Inspired by the Chinese side dish pai huang gua, this preparation highlights the cooling, refreshing qualities of cucumbers by smashing them! Now, any recipe that requires you to SMASH something is absolutely for me, but smashing the cucumbers also creates irregular shapes and really breaks up the flesh, so after the cucumber is salted and drained, the pieces act like tiny sponges for all the delicious sauce. If you're not a big fan of tedious knife work, this recipe is for you!

It's really important to use toasted sesame oil here; it's more richly flavored than regular sesame oil. It's also important to pick out a high-quality chili oil (I like Lao Gan Ma Spicy Chili Crisp or Fly by Jing Sichuan Chili Crisp, both available online), because it's a delicious, flavor-packed ingredient on its own, so a good one will bring even more flavor to the cucumbers. Finally, don't skip the fresh cilantro at the end. This dish is packed with bold flavors, so you need that freshness to balance everything perfectly.

2 large English cucumbers, ends trimmed

1 teaspoon kosher salt

1 teaspoon sugar

1 garlic clove, grated

1 teaspoon grated ginger (from a 1-inch piece of fresh ginger)

¼ cup soy sauce

3 tablespoons rice wine vinegar

2 teaspoons toasted sesame oil

2 teaspoons honey

2 tablespoons chili oil, plus more for finishing

1 tablespoon toasted sesame seeds

2 scallions, green and white parts, thinly sliced

Chopped fresh cilantro leaves, for garnish

1/ Cut each cucumber into three or four pieces crosswise, roughly 2 inches long, and then halve each piece lengthwise. Place the cucumber pieces cut-side down on a cutting board and, using the flat side of a large knife, carefully crush each piece until the skin cracks and the flesh is flattened. Place the cucumbers in a fine-mesh strainer set over a large bowl. Add the salt and sugar and toss to combine. Cover with a kitchen towel or a smaller bowl, then place something heavy on top, like a large can. Let sit for 15 to 20 minutes.

2/ While the cucumbers rest, make the dressing. In a large bowl, whisk together the garlic, ginger, soy sauce, rice wine vinegar, sesame oil, honey, and chili oil. Set aside.

3/ Discard any liquid from the cucumbers that has collected at the bottom of the bowl. Add the pressed cucumber flesh to the large bowl with the dressing and toss to coat. Top the salad with more chili oil to taste, the sesame seeds, scallions, and cilantro and serve.

Grilled Corn, Tomato & Halloumi Salad

WITH PESTO

● SERVES 4

This is a salad that proves you don't need meat to enjoy one of summer's best features: grilling! Halloumi is one of my favorite cheeses to use in the summer, because it's one of the only cheeses you can actually grill. And it's not the only grilled ingredient here: If you've never tried to grill fresh corn on the cob, it's 100 percent worth it; the heat brings out corn's natural sweetness, and the kernels char and develop a delicious smoky flavor that is impossible to re-create with frozen corn. That, combined with bursts of freshness from the tomatoes, the garlicky-herby pesto, and the salty cheese, make for something you'll want to bring to any summer get-together. You know those sad dishes at potlucks where there are only a few, polite spoonfuls missing? Yeah, this isn't one of those! It also travels well, so whether you're on a boat, at the beach, or on a camping trip, this dish will be your go-to.

BASIL PESTO

1½ cups fresh basil leaves (3 ounces), plus more for garnish

¼ cup pine nuts, toasted

⅓ cup freshly grated Parmesan cheese

1 teaspoon red wine vinegar

⅓ cup olive oil

Kosher salt and freshly ground black pepper

SALAD

4 large ears of corn, shucked

2 tablespoons olive oil

Kosher salt

8 ounces halloumi cheese, sliced into ½-inch-thick planks

1½ cups heirloom cherry tomatoes, halved

1 teaspoon red wine vinegar

Freshly ground black pepper

1/ **MAKE THE PESTO** In the bowl of a food processor or a high-speed blender, combine the basil, pine nuts, Parmesan, and vinegar. Turn the machine on then slowly stream in the oil until it's fully incorporated and smooth. Season to taste with the salt and pepper.

2/ **MAKE THE SALAD** Preheat a grill or grill pan to medium-high. Rub the corn with the oil and season with salt. Grill, rotating periodically, until all sides are charred, 8 to 10 minutes. Transfer the corn to a cutting board and let it cool slightly. Meanwhile, grill the halloumi until it's

golden brown on both sides, about 3 minutes per side. Set aside.

3/ When the corn and halloumi are cool enough to handle, slice the kernels off the cob and cut the grilled halloumi into bite-size pieces. Add the corn, halloumi, tomatoes, vinegar, and pesto to a large bowl and toss. Season to taste with salt and pepper, garnish with more basil, and serve.

Za'atar Roasted Acorn Squash

WITH GOAT CHEESE, PINE NUTS & POMEGRANATE MOLASSES

● SERVES 4 TO 6

The recipe is autumn in a bowl, so I hope you're reading this in October! It is heavily inspired by my mom: She loves fall and she might love squash even more. Every fall, she gets so excited when squash and pumpkins appear in the grocery store, and we incorporate them into as many meals as possible during the season. My mom also loves goat cheese and pomegranate, so this dish is not only a perfect combination of flavors and textures, it's also perfectly my mom.

Now, my favorite component of this dish has to be the za'atar, a Middle Eastern spice mix that includes the herb za'atar, along with a wide variety of things, such as sesame seeds, sumac, and salt. (Confusingly, *za'atar* can also refer to the plant itself, a lemony, peppery herb also known as wild thyme or hyssop.) It's a delicious, savory mix of flavors for almost any vegetable or protein you can think of, and it's so insanely good on the acorn squash!

---

3 medium acorn squash, ends trimmed, halved, seeded, and cut into 2-inch-thick wedges

5 tablespoons olive oil, plus more for finishing

1½ tablespoons za'atar spice blend

Kosher salt and freshly ground black pepper

¼ cup crumbled goat cheese

2 tablespoons pine nuts, toasted

2 tablespoons pomegranate molasses (available online and in specialty stores)

1 tablespoon chopped fresh parsley

Lemon wedges, for serving

1/ Preheat the oven to 425°F.

2/ Line two rimmed sheet pans with aluminum foil and evenly distribute the squash wedges between both pans. Drizzle the oil over the squash, then sprinkle the za'atar on top. Season with salt and pepper and toss to combine. Bake until deeply golden brown, 40 to 50 minutes, flipping the squash halfway through cooking.

3/ Transfer the cooked squash to a serving platter and top with the crumbled goat cheese, toasted pine nuts, pomegranate molasses, parsley, and additional olive oil. Serve immediately with lemon wedges.

QUICK BITE

I leave the skin on the acorn squash here for a few reasons. First, and most importantly, it saves preparation time! Second, the skin gets super crispy while the squash roasts, so it becomes almost like a squash-skin chip. That crunch is the perfect textural contrast to the tender squash and soft goat cheese.

Seared Brussels Sprouts

WITH CHILI DIJON PAN SAUCE

● SERVES 6

I have my friend Rachel Dolfi to thank for this one. After I spent a lifetime hating Brussels sprouts, Rachel cooked them for me once, and my mind was *blown*. For the first time ever, I not only liked Brussels sprouts, I LOVED them. Chances are, if you're reading this and think you also don't like Brussels sprouts, it's because you've never had them cooked to perfection, either. Here and now, I'm telling you that this recipe will win over even the biggest Brussels sprouts skeptic among us!

The key to a great sprout is the perfect cooking time. If they're under-cooked, they're tough and hard to eat, but if they're overcooked, they're super bitter. The cooking method and heat are important, too: When you cook them just right at high heat, either sautéing, roasting, or searing (as they are here), the natural sugars caramelize, so that the outer leaves get crisp and golden while the inside is perfectly tender.

---

4 tablespoons vegetable oil

2 pounds Brussels sprouts, ends trimmed and halved

Kosher salt

2 tablespoons olive oil

1 medium shallot, minced

3 garlic cloves, minced

2 tablespoons Dijon mustard

1 teaspoon honey

4 to 6 jarred Calabrian chilies, sliced (see Quick Bite)

1 cup vegetable stock

Juice of ½ lemon

Lemon zest, for garnish

Freshly ground black pepper

1/ In a large skillet set over medium-high heat, add 2 tablespoons of the vegetable oil. When it's hot and shimmering, add half of the Brussels sprouts, cut-side down. Season with salt and sear for 3 to 4 minutes, flipping halfway through, then cook for an additional 3 to 4 minutes, until golden brown. Remove from the heat and transfer the sprouts to a large heatproof bowl. Add the remaining 2 tablespoons vegetable oil to the skillet and repeat the process with the second batch of Brussels sprouts.

2/ Reduce the heat to medium and, to the same skillet, add the olive oil, shallot, and garlic. Season with a pinch of salt and stir to combine. Sweat the shallot and garlic for 2 minutes, or until they become translucent and fragrant. Add the mustard and honey and stir continuously, incorporating the mustard with the shallot and garlic. Cook for 30 seconds to 1 minute, then add the sliced chilies (4 for less heat, 6 for more heat) and cook for an additional 30 seconds. Pour in the vegetable

stock and lemon juice and stir to combine. Bring to a boil and cook for 2 to 3 minutes, until the liquid has thickened slightly.

3/ Add the Brussels sprouts back to the pan and toss with tongs to fully combine. Simmer for 2 to 3 minutes, until the Brussels sprouts have absorbed some of the liquid.

4/ For serving, transfer the Brussels sprouts to a serving platter and garnish with lemon zest and black pepper. Serve immediately.

QUICK BITE

If you aren't sure where to buy Calabrian chilies or can't find them in your grocery store, they're fairly easy to find online! That said, if you're in a pinch or don't have time to wait for some to arrive in the mail, pickled cherry peppers will work just fine.

Loaded Roasted Cauliflower

● SERVES 4 TO 6

As a little kid, I was insanely picky, especially about vegetables. I really wouldn't eat a single one except for potatoes, and I think we can question how much those really count given their fairly minimal nutritional value. (To be clear, this is *not* potato slander; it's well documented in this book that they are still my favorite, but we have to be honest about what they bring to the table in terms of nutrition.) Cauliflower was the first vegetable I ever liked after potatoes, and this recipe is my favorite way to eat it.

Israel is known to many as a capital of cauliflower innovation, so in my opinion, the best way to eat it is to pair it with Middle Eastern ingredients and flavors. Also, the key to great cauliflower, for any of you cauliflower skeptics out there, is to make sure it's roasted or sautéed; you want a crispy, brown exterior and a tender—but not mushy!—interior. Assembling this dish always feels like an art project to me, because the toppings are so colorful: There's a hefty drizzle of tahini for nutty flavor and creamy texture, dill and mint for herby freshness and pops of green, pistachios for crunch, and lots of pomegranate seeds for bursts of tang and acidity, plus a beautiful, deep red color.

1 head of cauliflower, cut into small florets (about 4 cups)

¼ cup extra-virgin olive oil

Zest and juice of 2 lemons

1 tablespoon za'atar spice blend, plus more for garnish

1 teaspoon kosher salt

½ teaspoon freshly ground black pepper

⅓ cup well-stirred tahini

¼ cup pomegranate seeds

2 tablespoons chopped pistachios

2 tablespoons chopped fresh dill

2 tablespoons chopped fresh mint

1/ Preheat the oven to 450°F.

2/ In a large bowl, combine the cauliflower, olive oil, the zest and juice of 1 lemon, the za'atar, salt, and pepper and toss. Evenly distribute the cauliflower between two rimmed sheet pans. Roast the cauliflower, flipping the florets over halfway through, until it's deeply golden brown, 35 to 45 minutes.

3/ Transfer the cauliflower to a serving plate. Top with the zest and juice of the remaining lemon and drizzle with the tahini. Sprinkle with the pomegranate seeds, pistachios, dill, mint, and additional za'atar. Serve warm.

QUICK BITE

Like most of the recipes in this book, if you are missing any ingredients or want to play around with different flavors, feel free to add any of your other favorite toppings or spices! This cauliflower would be great with toasted pine nuts, roasted chickpeas, or even crumbled feta cheese or labneh. Anything from Middle Eastern cuisine will pair beautifully, so definitely feel free to experiment!

Triple Pea Salad

WITH CRUNCHY FARRO

● SERVES 6

Although I've come very far in my vegetable-consumption journey since my days of only eating potatoes, I still tend toward ones that are on the beige and brown end of the color spectrum. (Hello, cauliflower!) This dish has been a gateway recipe for me to the greener side of things. Having different textures that play off each other in a dish is what really elevates the eating experience, and this recipe might win the "Best Texture" award for this whole book. The fresh peas are perfectly crisp, while the fried farro adds incredible crunch. (And yes, there's a difference between crispy and crunchy!) A salad that somehow has no lettuce in it is the salad for me!

½ cup uncooked farro

⅓ cup extra-virgin olive oil

¼ cup sherry vinegar

¼ cup fresh parsley leaves, tightly packed

2 tablespoons chopped fresh oregano leaves

2 tablespoons chopped fresh basil leaves

2 garlic cloves, minced

Kosher salt and freshly ground black pepper

1 cup frozen peas

Neutral oil, for frying

1 (6-ounce) package snow peas (about 2 packed cups), ends trimmed and destringed and cut on the bias into ½-inch pieces

1 (6-ounce) package sugar snap peas (about 2 packed cups), ends trimmed and cut on the bias into ½-inch pieces

Shaved Parmesan cheese, for garnish

1/ Line a small sheet pan with paper towels and set aside. Cook the farro according to the package directions, drain well, and spread out on the prepared sheet pan. Set aside in the refrigerator for at least 1 hour to slightly dry out, or up to overnight.

2/ In a large bowl, whisk together the olive oil, sherry vinegar, parsley, oregano, basil, and garlic to combine. Taste and season with salt and pepper. Set the vinaigrette aside to let the flavors marry.

3/ Add the peas to a microwave-safe bowl and microwave for 2 to 3 minutes, or until slightly warm to the touch. Line another small sheet pan with paper towels. Transfer the cooked peas to the lined sheet pan and roll them around on the paper towels until most of the moisture has been soaked up. Place in the refrigerator until ready to use.

4/ In a medium skillet, add ½ inch of neutral oil and heat to 400°F. Line another small sheet pan with paper towels while the oil is preheating. Add the farro and gently stir it with a slotted spoon to ensure the farro does not clump together. Cook for 90 seconds, or until the farro turns a deeper golden color. Remove with a slotted spoon and transfer to the prepared sheet pan. Season with salt and set aside to cool.

5/ Once the farro has cooled, add it to the large bowl with the vinaigrette, along with the snow peas, sugar snap peas, and cooked peas. Toss to combine and transfer the salad to a serving bowl. Add shaved Parmesan over the top and serve immediately.

QUICK BITE

The salad keeps very well, but the farro tends to act like little sponges that soak up all the vinaigrette quicker than the other ingredients, so the texture will be off. If you're making this ahead, reserve half the dressing to mix in right before serving.

SOUF

Of all the chapters in this book, this one is by far the most nostalgic for me. It's filled with recipes that are either directly from or inspired by the most important people in my life. You might say this collection is a family affair: everyone in my family, including my grandmas, has made a contribution to this chapter. #BernathsRepresent!!!

More than any other type of food, soups and stews embody what comfort food is. When you cook them, the aroma fills your entire house, and a bowl of soup feels like an edible hug. They make cold days warmer, sad days happier, and sick days easier. I can't imagine anything more comforting than that!

Soups and stews tend to have reputations for being hot, heavy meals with long cook times, but this collection of recipes will show you that you don't need to wait for winter or a long weekend to dive into this chapter. I do have that kind of recipe, so if you want something that'll really stick to your ribs, try the **Smoky Short Rib & White Bean Stew** on page 150. I also have elevated versions of some classics, like the **Triple Tomato Soup with Cheesy Garlic Bread** on page 148. But I've included lighter, superfast soups here, too, like **Yoni's Strawberry Soup** (page 159) and my **Gazpacho** (page 154). And because these recipes often get their amazing flavor from simmering or chilling different ingredients together, you get great payoff with minimal effort on your part. If you don't have much experience in the kitchen, this chapter is a great place to start.

S AND STEWS

Grandma's Chicken Soup

● **SERVES 10 TO 12**

We all know that everyone thinks their grandma makes the best chicken soup, so it won't surprise you to know that my grandma Linda makes THE BEST chicken soup, and if you disagree, you're wrong! That said, one thing we can all agree on is that the most important ingredient in any chicken soup recipe is love. And mine is full of it.

My grandma makes this for the High Holidays and at Passover. This two-day recipe has all the classic flavors: chicken, carrots, celery root, parsnip, and fresh herbs. Of course, the star of the show is the matzo balls. Matzo balls fall into two categories—dense and fluffy—and people are usually loyal to one. It is a tradition in my family, passed down from my paternal great-grandfather to my father, to make dense matzo balls, and here in this book, I'm ready to take on all the dense matzo ball haters that I haven't converted already. My matzo balls have a texture that is chewy but still tender, and they don't disintegrate into the broth, so you can get a bit of each ingredient in every spoonful.

SOUP

1 (5-pound) chicken, cut into 8 pieces, or an assortment of chicken pieces (thighs, drums, breasts, wings)

6 carrots, halved lengthwise, then cut crosswise into 3-inch lengths

4 garlic cloves

1 large onion, quartered

1 small parsnip, peeled, quartered lengthwise, then cut crosswise into 3-inch lengths

½ medium turnip, peeled and cut into ¼-inch slices

½ celery root, peeled and cut into ¼-inch slices

1 small bunch fresh flat-leaf parsley

1 small bunch fresh curly parsley

½ bunch fresh dill

2 pounds chicken bones or chicken wings

Kosher salt

1 tablespoon sweet paprika

Freshly ground black pepper

MATZO BALLS

3 cups matzo meal

1 cup seltzer

7 large eggs

2 tablespoons schmaltz (rendered chicken fat) or vegetable oil

1 tablespoon kosher salt

2 teaspoons freshly ground black pepper

1/ MAKE THE SOUP Pierce the chicken pieces all over with a fork. (This will allow the broth to penetrate the meat.) Set aside. Repeat with the carrots, garlic, onion, parsnip, turnip, and celery root, piercing them all over to allow the broth to penetrate the vegetables.

2/ In a large stockpot, place the vegetables, then the herbs on top, followed by the chicken bones, and finally the chicken pieces. Add salt and enough cold water to cover everything by 1 inch. Bring to a boil over high heat, then reduce the heat to medium-low and cook,

undisturbed, for 1 hour. Remove from the heat, add the paprika and pepper to taste, give the pot a gentle stir, and let it cool for 45 minutes.

3/ Using tongs, remove the chicken, vegetables, and herbs from the pot and set them aside to cool. Strain the chicken stock through a colander into a large resealable container (or divide it between two containers) to remove any large solids, but keep the smaller bits in the stock. Discard the large solids.

4/ Place the stock in the refrigerator to chill overnight. When the chicken has cooled enough to handle it, remove and discard the chicken skin and bones, then shred the meat into medium pieces. Package the chicken, vegetables, and herbs separately in three different containers and refrigerate them as well.

5/ The next day, pour half of the stock (or as much as you want to use) back into a large stockpot and begin to reheat it over medium-low heat. Return the rest of the stock to the refrigerator.

6/ MAKE THE MATZO BALLS While the soup is reheating, bring a large saucepot of water to a boil. While you wait for the water to boil, combine all the matzo ball ingredients in a large bowl and stir to combine. Measure out ¼ cup of the mixture and roll it into a ball using your hands; set aside. Repeat until you have formed as many matzo balls as you want to cook (usually 2 or 3 per person; see Quick Bite), then add the matzo balls to the pot and boil until cooked through, about 15 minutes. (To see if the matzo balls are done, remove a ball from the pot and cut it in half to check that the insides are cooked.) Remove the cooked matzo balls with a slotted spoon and transfer to a plate.

7/ Five minutes before serving, add half of the chicken and vegetables (or as much as you want to serve) and a few sprigs of cooked herbs to the chicken stock, just to warm them through. Taste and adjust the seasoning with salt and pepper to your liking.

8/ Using a slotted spoon, evenly distribute the chicken, vegetables, and herbs among five or six serving bowls. Place 2 or 3 matzo balls in each bowl, pour stock over, and serve immediately.

QUICK BITE

This recipe makes up to 12 servings, but you don't have to eat it all at once! My grandmother usually serves this recipe to our family over two holiday meals, but you can divide it however you like. (Once cooked, the stock, chicken, vegetables, and herbs will keep in the refrigerator for up to 5 days. The uncooked matzo ball mix will keep in the refrigerator for a day.)

Mushroom Bobo

Rosa Alves, who has known me since I was eight months old and is incredibly near and dear to my family, is the source for this amazing recipe. One day while developing recipes for this book, I found myself with more beautiful local mushrooms than I could use, and I really didn't want them to go to waste. So I went to Rosa for some inspiration, and she told me about one of her family's favorite recipes: shrimp bobo. Rosa, who is Brazilian, shared that the dish is associated with the city of Salvador in the Brazilian state of Bahia, so it is heavily influenced by the large West African and Afro-Brazilian populations there. She described it as a mix between chowder and stew and said that we could easily substitute all those extra mushrooms I had for the shrimp. We made it together that day, by which I mean Rosa made it and I took notes and asked a hundred questions along the way. Between the rich yuca base, creamy coconut milk, and ginger, garlic, and lime flavors throughout, it's a hearty, filling meal that somehow won't make a nap afterward necessary. I'm so honored to be able to share her bobo recipe in my book.

3 large pieces of frozen root yuca (see Quick Bite)

3 tablespoons olive oil

1 large yellow onion, chopped

1 small red bell pepper, chopped

1 jalapeño, chopped

Kosher salt

3 medium Roma tomatoes, roughly chopped

2 garlic cloves, roughly chopped

1 (1-inch) piece fresh ginger, peeled and roughly chopped

1½ cups chicken or vegetable stock

1 (13.5-ounce) can full-fat coconut milk, shaken

1 tablespoon soy sauce

Juice of 1 lime

2 teaspoons hot sauce, such as Tabasco

1 tablespoon vegetable oil

1 pound mushrooms, such as oyster or cremini, stemmed and cut into 2-inch pieces

Chopped fresh cilantro leaves, for garnish

1/ In a large saucepot, cover the yuca with water. Bring to a boil over high heat, then reduce the heat to low and cook until very tender, about 15 minutes. Drain, then set aside to cool.

2/ Meanwhile, heat a large Dutch oven over medium-high heat and add 2 tablespoons of the olive oil. Once hot and shimmering, add the onion, bell pepper, and jalapeño. Season with salt and stir to combine. Cook until the onion softens and the edges begin to caramelize, 6 to 8 minutes. Add the tomatoes, garlic, and ginger and cook until fragrant, about 1 minute. Add the stock, bring to a boil, then reduce the heat to medium. Simmer until slightly reduced and thickened, about 10 minutes. Working in batches, carefully transfer the mixture to a high-powered blender, filling it up no more than three-quarters, and blend until the mixture is completely puréed. Once it's smooth, transfer to a heatproof bowl and repeat with the remaining vegetables. Cover the soup with a lid to keep it warm.

3/ Once the yuca is cool enough to handle, remove the yellow core and grate the yuca on the second largest holes of a box grater. Measure out 1½ cups of the yuca and set it aside.

4/ Wipe out the Dutch oven with a paper towel, then return to the stove. Set over medium heat, add the remaining 1 tablespoon olive oil, then stir in the grated yuca. Sauté for 2 to 3 minutes to allow the yuca to release its moisture, then whisk in all but 2 tablespoons

recipe continues

of the coconut milk (reserving the rest) and continue whisking until the coconut and yuca form a thick paste, about 2 minutes. Once the mixture has thickened, pour in the reserved vegetable purée and stir to combine. Add the soy sauce, lime juice, and hot sauce and stir to combine. Reduce the heat to low and gently simmer for 10 minutes.

5/ While the soup is simmering, set a medium skillet over medium-high heat. Add the vegetable oil and, once it's hot and shimmering, add half of the mushrooms and sear them, undisturbed, until deeply golden brown, 2 to 4 minutes. Flip and repeat on the other side. Transfer the mushrooms to a plate and season with salt. Repeat with the remaining mushrooms.

6/ Ladle the soup into four bowls. Top with the mushrooms, reserved coconut milk, and cilantro. Serve immediately.

QUICK BITE

I call for frozen yuca because it's usually easier to find than fresh. If you do have access to fresh yuca and would like to use it, just peel it, boil it in salted water until tender (30 to 45 minutes), and then carry on with the recipe as written! Also, I'd be remiss if I didn't say that bobo is often served over rice, so if you'd like to make this a more substantial meal, ladling the stew over freshly cooked white rice is absolutely delicious.

Hearty Tomatillo Beef Stew

● SERVES 4 TO 6

If you're craving salty, hearty, umami savoriness, this is the recipe for you! It is my re-creation of carne en su jugo (literally meaning "meat cooked in its juice"), a rich and flavorful beef soup from Mexico. While it's not short on protein (between the meat and pinto beans), it's also spiced with tomatillos, jalapeño, cumin, and chili powder and finished with lots of fresh lime juice and cilantro, so the final dish is rich and filling but also packed with flavor. This is a real stick-to-your-ribs kind of soup, but it's also short on cook time, so it's perfect for entertaining, because you can whip it up quickly and be sure no one will leave your table hungry.

6 bacon slices (I use beef bacon), cut into ½-inch pieces

1½ pounds flank or skirt steak, cut into ½-inch pieces

Kosher salt and freshly ground black pepper

8 ounces fresh tomatillos, husked, cored, and cut into wedges

½ cup fresh cilantro leaves, plus more for garnish

½ large yellow onion, cut into wedges

3 large garlic cloves

2 medium jalapeños, chopped

1 teaspoon ground cumin

½ teaspoon chili powder

2 cups beef stock

2 (15-ounce) cans pinto beans, drained and rinsed

2 teaspoons soy sauce

1 tablespoon lime juice

Chopped red onion and thinly sliced radishes, for garnish

Lime wedges, for serving

1/ In a large pot or Dutch oven set over medium heat, cook the bacon until the fat has rendered and the bacon has crisped, 13 to 15 minutes. Using a slotted spoon, remove the bacon from the pan, leaving the rendered fat behind; set the bacon aside.

2/ Season the steak with salt and pepper and add it to the same pot you cooked the bacon in. Increase the heat to medium-high and sauté until the beef is cooked through, but not browned, 4 to 6 minutes.

3/ While the beef is cooking, combine the tomatillos, cilantro, onion, garlic, jalapeño, cumin, and chili powder in a high-speed blender or in the bowl of a food processor. Blend until smooth.

4/ Add the tomatillo mixture to the pot, followed by the stock, beans, soy sauce, and lime juice. Bring the soup to a boil, then reduce the heat to medium-low and cook until slightly reduced, about 10 minutes.

5/ To serve, ladle the soup into bowls. Divide the bacon between them, then garnish each bowl with some chopped onion, radish slices, and cilantro leaves. Serve immediately, with lime wedges on the side.

Chicken & Mushroom Ramen

WITH THAI GREEN CURRY

● SERVES 2

Back in 2016, I met Josh Reisner through Instagram, and we quickly developed a friendship based on our shared obsession with cooking and passion for food from cuisines all over the world. (Josh's dad is an Ashkenazi Jew and his mom is from Singapore.) When we finally got to cook together, this ramen was what we made.

Growing up in Queens, New York, Josh's parents preferred bringing him with them when they went out to eat rather than leaving him at home, so from a very young age, he got to try lots of incredible food. That inspired him to learn to cook himself—a feeling I can definitely relate to! Josh started working with kitchen mentors, including some from Japan, and through them, he learned about the history and traditions behind this dish before he started making his own ramen at age eleven. What Josh loves about ramen is how you can use the basic components—noodles, tare, broth, oil, and toppings—and combine them with tastes and dishes from other cuisines to create ramen homages to any kind of food. When we cooked together, he said that if someone described their day, he could design a bowl of ramen around it, using those five components to represent the different parts of their story.

I learned some important things about three of these components from Josh that I'm excited to share with you here. First, the oil is super important because it boosts the olfactory element, so it drives your first impression of the bowl. This particular ramen uses garlic oil, so the first thing you smell is toasty, garlicky goodness. Second, you must use ramen noodles, because they contain an ingredient called kansui, an alkaline substance that's mixed into the dough and gives ramen noodles their signature chewy texture. Finally, there's the tare, which is essentially ramen's concentrated flavoring or seasoning agent. Because the elements are prepared separately, you can make sure each one is perfect before you combine them, which makes for a truly exceptional, and personalized, bowl of ramen.

BROTH

2 skin-on, bone-in chicken thighs

1 tablespoon Thai green curry paste

1 tablespoon vegetable oil

4 ears of corn, shucked

8 scallions, green and white parts, thinly sliced

1 red onion, cut into large chunks (about 1½ cups)

½ cup mirin (rice wine)

6 cups chicken stock

8 dried shiitake mushrooms

Reserved mushroom stems

MUSHROOMS

Vegetable oil

1½ cups assorted fresh mushrooms, sliced, such as oyster and shiitake, stems trimmed and reserved for the broth

Pinch of granulated sugar

2 tablespoons mirin (rice wine)

Kosher salt

TARE

4 teaspoons vegetable oil

2 tablespoons grated fresh ginger

2 tablespoons grated garlic

4 tablespoons soy sauce

4 teaspoons dark brown sugar

2 scallions (white and green parts kept separate), thinly sliced

2 (4-ounce) portions fresh ramen noodles, or 2 (3-ounce) packages dried noodles

recipe continues

1/ MAKE THE BROTH Remove the chicken thighs from the refrigerator and massage the green curry paste all over the chicken. Allow the chicken to sit at room temperature for 1 hour.

2/ In a large stockpot set over medium-high heat, add the oil. Once it's hot and shimmering, add the corn and sear on all sides for 8 minutes total. Transfer the corn to a cutting board and let cool slightly. Once it's cool enough to handle, cut off the kernels, reserving the cobs, and set them aside in a small bowl.

3/ In the same pot set over medium-high heat, add the marinated chicken, skin-side down, and sear on each side until golden brown, about 3 minutes per side. Remove the chicken from the pot and set aside.

4/ To the same pot, add the scallions and red onion and cook until the onion is thoroughly charred, about 2 minutes. Stir in the mirin and cook for 1 minute, or until reduced by half. Add the chicken thighs, reserved corn cobs, stock, 6 cups water, dried shiitakes, and reserved mushroom stems. Raise the heat to high, bring to a light boil, then reduce the heat to medium and cook uncovered for 90 minutes, or until reduced by a third.

5/ PREPARE THE MUSHROOMS While the broth is cooking, in a small nonstick skillet set over medium-high heat, add a drop of oil, then add the mushrooms and cook until golden brown, about 2 minutes. Flip and season them with the granulated sugar, mirin, and salt

and cook for an additional 1 to 2 minutes, until the mushrooms are golden brown and glazed on both sides. Transfer the mushrooms to a bowl.

6/ MAKE THE TARE In the same small skillet set over medium heat, combine the oil, ginger, and garlic. Sauté until fragrant and lightly golden brown, about 1 minute. Remove from the heat and divide evenly between two large bowls. Divide the soy sauce, brown sugar, and scallion whites between each serving bowl. Set aside.

7/ Once the broth is done cooking, remove the chicken thighs from the pot and set them aside to cool. Discard the skin and bones and, using a fork or clean hands, shred the meat into ¼- to ½-inch-thick strands. Set aside.

8/ Carefully strain the remaining liquid from the pot through a fine-mesh strainer into a heatproof bowl. Discard the solids, then return the liquid to the pot and cover with a lid to keep warm.

9/ Bring a large pot of water to a boil. Add the ramen noodles, cook according to the package directions, or until they're soft but still have some tooth to them, and drain.

10/ To assemble, divide the ramen noodles between the two bowls, placing them on top of the tare. Pour in the broth, dividing it evenly between the bowls, then add the chicken and mushrooms, and garnish with the corn kernels and scallion greens. Serve immediately.

Turkish Red Lentil Soup

● SERVES 6

There are times when I want big, complex, in-your-face flavors, but other times I think simple flavors, cooked perfectly, are just as tasty. Not every recipe has to have layers and layers of seasoning and flavor to be delicious! This soup, based on a Turkish soup called mercimek çorbasi, is made with just a few ingredients and tastes like nourishment in a bowl. While it's unquestionably a comfort food, it is still simple and light. After the hot soup is ladled into bowls, each serving is topped with half a lemon's worth of fresh juice, and the brightness and acidity of that garnish is the key to the final mouthwatering product.

This soup is also, coincidentally, gluten-free and vegan. (My mom is gluten-free, and she loves this dish!) So this recipe is also perfect for when you need to serve a crowd of mixed diets; I'm certain that everyone from vegans to carnivores will leave the table full and happy!

2 tablespoons olive oil, plus more for drizzling

1 medium yellow onion, chopped

2 medium carrots, chopped

Kosher salt and freshly ground black pepper

2 large garlic cloves, chopped

1 tablespoon tomato paste

1½ cups red lentils, rinsed and drained

1 teaspoon Aleppo pepper, plus more for serving (see Quick Bite)

¼ teaspoon ground cumin

Dried mint, for serving

2 lemons, halved, for serving

1/ In a large saucepot set over medium heat, add the oil, onion, carrots, and a pinch of salt. Stir to combine and sweat until the onion is translucent and the carrots are beginning to soften, 6 to 7 minutes. Season with salt and black pepper. Add the garlic and cook until fragrant, about 1 minute. Add the tomato paste, stir to combine, and cook until the tomato paste turns a dark brick-red color, stirring almost continuously, 2 to 3 minutes. Fold in the dried lentils, Aleppo pepper, and cumin. Cook for 1 to 2 minutes, toasting the spices and the lentils. Add 6 cups water, increase to medium-high heat and bring to a boil, then reduce the heat to medium-low. Cover and simmer for 20 minutes, or until the lentils are soft and tender.

2/ Working in batches, carefully transfer the soup to a blender, being careful not to fill it more than three-quarters of the way. (You can also remove the cap from the top of the blender and cover it with a kitchen towel to prevent the top from popping off.) Blend until a smooth, thin consistency forms, 30 seconds to 1 minute, then transfer to a heatproof bowl and repeat with the remaining batches. Return the puréed soup to the pot and simmer over medium-low heat for an additional 20 minutes, stirring occasionally, or until the mixture has slightly thickened. Season to taste with salt and black pepper.

3/ To serve, divide the soup among six bowls. Top each bowl with a drizzle of olive oil, additional Aleppo pepper, dried mint, and the juice of half a lemon.

QUICK BITE
If you don't have Aleppo pepper, substitute ½ teaspoon each of sweet paprika and crushed red pepper flakes.

Triple Tomato Soup

WITH CHEESY GARLIC BREAD

● SERVES 6 TO 8

Tomato soup with grilled cheese is the textbook definition of comfort food, so when I was creating this recipe, I didn't try to fix something that isn't even a little bit broken. Instead, my goal was to enhance it. I found I got the most intense tomato flavor by adding roasted red peppers and sun-dried tomatoes to the soup. To up the depth of flavor even further, I added fresh basil, lots of garlic, and just a touch of heavy cream.

My cheesy garlic bread is like a grilled-cheese-garlic-bread crouton that you can dip right into the tomato goodness, and I especially love that it comes together quickly under the broiler. The Gruyère gets perfectly bubbly and golden in just a couple of minutes. Canned tomato soup and grilled cheese be warned—you've got serious competition.

SOUP

2 tablespoons unsalted butter

2 tablespoons olive oil

1 large yellow onion, chopped

2 garlic cloves, chopped

2 tablespoons chopped sun-dried tomatoes

2 tablespoons all-purpose flour

3 tablespoons tomato paste

2 (28-ounce) cans whole peeled tomatoes

1 cup vegetable stock

½ cup chopped roasted red pepper from a jar or homemade

½ teaspoon crushed red pepper flakes

2 teaspoons fresh thyme leaves

Kosher salt and freshly ground black pepper

½ cup heavy cream

8 fresh basil leaves

CHEESY GARLIC BREAD

1 baguette, cut into ½-inch-thick slices on an extreme bias

½ stick salted butter, melted

4 garlic cloves, finely chopped

8 ounces Gruyère cheese, grated

Fresh thyme leaves, for garnish

1/ **MAKE THE SOUP** In a large pot or Dutch oven, heat the butter and olive oil over medium-low heat. Add the chopped onion and cook until soft and translucent, about 8 minutes. Add the garlic and sun-dried tomatoes and cook until fragrant, about 1 minute. Add the flour and stir until the mixture is slightly thickened and pale golden, about 2 minutes, being sure not to brown the mixture. Stir in the tomato paste and cook until it turns brick red, 2 to 4 minutes. Stir in the tomatoes, stock, roasted red peppers, red pepper flakes, and thyme. Taste and season with salt and black pepper. Raise the heat to medium-high and bring the soup to a light boil, then reduce the heat to medium-low and cook for about 25 minutes, tasting, until the flavors have married, stirring the bottom of the pot frequently.

2/ Remove the pot from the heat and stir in the heavy cream and basil. Working in batches, carefully transfer the soup to a high-powered blender, filling it up no more than three-quarters of the way, and blend until the soup is completely puréed. (You can also remove the cap from the top of the blender and cover it with a kitchen towel to prevent the lid from popping off.) Once it's smooth, transfer to a heatproof bowl and repeat with the remaining soup, then return the puréed soup to the pot, and cover to keep it warm. (Alternatively, you can blend the soup in the pot using an immersion blender.)

3/ **MAKE THE GARLIC BREAD** Preheat the broiler to high. Arrange the bread slices on a sheet pan in a single layer. Mix the melted butter and garlic together in a small bowl and slather the tops of the bread with the mixture. Top each bread slice with some of the Gruyère and broil until bubbly and golden brown, 3 to 5 minutes. Top with fresh thyme leaves.

4/ Divide the soup among bowls and serve immediately, with the hot bread alongside.

Smoky Short Rib & White Bean Stew

● SERVES 6 TO 8

This stew was heavily inspired by and adapted from traditional Spanish fabada, a rich, hearty stew typically served during the winter, at lunch, which was typically the main meal of the day. Fabada broth is packed with white beans, pork shoulder, chorizo, and bacon, but in my version, I sub beef short ribs for the pork shoulder. I use short ribs because they give the soup the same low-and-slow shredded meat texture.

What I love most about this recipe is how deeply savory and filling it is. I usually serve it as a main course, and I make sure to plan a few hours of sitting around and doing nothing afterward. It's the perfect dinner after a long day outside in the cold or lunch on a snow day. Between the chorizo, saffron, and smoked paprika, the layers of flavor in this soup only get better over time, so it's a good candidate for a make-ahead project, or when you want something that will freeze well for later. No matter when you eat it, I guarantee you won't be hungry afterward!

2 tablespoons olive oil

2 pounds boneless beef short ribs, cut into 2-inch pieces

Kosher salt

1 (7-ounce) piece Spanish chorizo (I use beef chorizo), cut into ½-inch-thick half-moons

1 medium yellow onion, finely chopped

1 head garlic, outer layer removed, halved crosswise

2 tablespoons tomato paste

1 tablespoon smoked paprika

Pinch of saffron threads

1½ cups dried large white beans, such as cannellini, lupini, or white lima beans

6 cups chicken stock

Freshly ground black pepper

1/ In a large Dutch oven set over medium heat, add the oil. Season the beef with salt and, once the oil is hot and lightly shimmering, add half of the beef to the pot. Sear until golden brown, 3 to 4 minutes, then flip and repeat on the other side. Transfer to a plate and repeat with the remaining beef. Set aside.

2/ Reduce the heat to medium-low and add the chorizo. Cook until crisp, 2 to 3 minutes, then flip and repeat on the other side. Transfer to the plate and set aside.

3/ Add the onion and garlic halves, cut-side down, and season with a pinch of salt. Stir the onion to incorporate it into the fat and sauté until the onion becomes translucent and soft, 4 to 5 minutes. (Try to leave the garlic halves undisturbed so that the cut sides can brown.) Add the tomato paste and paprika and stir to completely coat the onion. Continue to stir occasionally, moving the tomato paste around to prevent it from burning. Cook for 2 to 3 minutes, until the tomato paste turns a dark brick-red color. Return the short ribs and chorizo to the Dutch oven, along with the saffron, dried beans, stock, pepper, and 2 cups water. Stir to combine. Bring to a boil, then reduce the heat to low and simmer uncovered until the beans have cooked through and the beef is fork-tender, 2½ to 3 hours. (Check occasionally to make sure the liquid has not dropped much below the meat and beans. If more liquid is needed during cooking, add additional water, preferably boiling or very hot.) Divide the soup equally among bowls and serve.

French Onion Soup

Like many classic French recipes (see the Crème Brûlée for Every Season on page 206), French onion soup can seem intimidating to home cooks. But I'm here to tell you that good French onion soup needs only one important thing, and that's *time*. If you can slice onions, use a measuring cup, and have an hour or so to stir, then you can make perfect, delicious, authentic French onion soup in your kitchen. The most essential ingredient (besides, you know, onions!) is a nice dry white wine. It serves two crucial functions: It cuts the sweetness of the jammy onions, and it deglazes the pot so that all the delicious flavor-packed brown bits of onion (called fond) from the caramelizing process come up off the bottom of the pot and get mixed into the soup. Like the crème brûlée, this recipe is also perfect for dinner guests, because not only is it impressive, but you can make it well ahead of time. (I'd argue it actually tastes better the longer it simmers so the flavors can marry!)

½ stick unsalted butter

3 tablespoons olive oil

6 large onions, thinly sliced into half-moons (10 to 12 cups)

2 large shallots, thinly sliced

4 garlic cloves, finely chopped

1 teaspoon sugar

Kosher salt and freshly ground black pepper

3 tablespoons all-purpose flour

¾ cup dry white wine

2 tablespoons white wine vinegar

3 fresh thyme sprigs

1 bay leaf

8 cups vegetable or beef stock (I use vegetable)

8 (¼-inch-thick) slices French bread, toasted

8 ounces Gruyère cheese, grated

1 teaspoon fresh thyme leaves, for garnish

1/ In a large heavy-bottomed pot or Dutch oven, melt the butter over medium-high heat. Add the olive oil, onions, shallots, garlic, sugar, and salt and pepper to taste and reduce the heat to medium. Cook, stirring occasionally, until the onions are softened, dark brown, and caramelized, 40 to 50 minutes. Sprinkle the flour over the onions, mix until combined, then cook until the flour mixture is fully incorporated and the onions have a slightly nutty smell, 2 to 3 minutes, stirring frequently to ensure nothing burns. Add the white wine and vinegar, scraping up any browned bits on the bottom of the pot. Increase the heat to medium-high and bring the mixture to a boil, then reduce it to medium-low and cook until the liquid has slightly reduced, about 3 minutes.

2/ Tie the thyme sprigs and bay leaf together with kitchen twine, add the sachet to the pot, and stir in the stock. Increase the heat to medium-high and bring to a boil, then reduce to low and simmer, stirring occasionally, until the soup has thickened, 35 to 40 minutes. Remove from the heat and discard the herb sachet.

3/ Preheat the oven to 450°F. Place four ovenproof bowls on a large, rimmed sheet pan. Divide the soup among the bowls, top each with 2 slices of bread (cut to fit if necessary), and sprinkle the grated cheese over the bread. Place in the oven and bake until the cheese is bubbling and golden brown, 6 to 8 minutes. Carefully remove the sheet pan from the oven and top the bowls with the fresh thyme leaves. Serve immediately.

QUICK BITE

If you don't have ovenproof bowls, you can keep the soup warm in the pot and toast the cheesy bread separately. Arrange the bread slices on a sheet pan, top with grated cheese, and broil until melted and bubbling, about 3 minutes. Place 2 toasts on each bowl of soup and serve.

Gazpacho

● SERVES 4 TO 6

This recipe is a special one for my mom and especially for her mom, my grandma Bobbie. When my mom was growing up, it was just the two of them, as my grandma was a single mother. My mom describes her as strong, super independent, and hardworking during those years.

One thing that they didn't have time or money for was traveling, so my grandma tried to expose my mom to the world through food and cooking. One recipe (which actually came from an old *Cosmopolitan* magazine) that quickly became one of their favorites was gazpacho. My grandma lost the original recipe a long time ago, so over the years, she made up her own. I have so many happy memories of visiting her as a kid and being served this soup, so now, as an ode to her ingenuity, I've taken her recipe and made it my own, too. This gazpacho, which includes a mix of tomatoes, vegetables, and vinegar, comes together perfectly through blending and chilling. It is so easy to make (a real throw-it-all-in-the-blender kind of recipe) and doesn't require that you turn on the stove, so it's perfect for a hot summer day. If you only think of soups as time-consuming projects for the winter months, I guarantee this will change your mind!

1 (28-ounce) can whole peeled tomatoes

1 Persian cucumber, cut into large pieces

1 red bell pepper, cut into large pieces

1 yellow bell pepper, cut into large pieces

1 medium jalapeño, cut into large pieces

1 small shallot, roughly chopped

¼ cup sherry vinegar

½ teaspoon sugar, or more to taste

Kosher salt and freshly ground black pepper

⅓ cup extra-virgin olive oil, plus more for serving

1/ In a high-powered blender or food processor, combine all the ingredients, adding salt and black pepper to taste, except for the olive oil. Process until the mixture resembles a chunky salsa. Then, on low speed, slowly stream in the olive oil. Taste and adjust with additional salt, black pepper, and sugar, as needed.

2/ Transfer the mixture to a resealable container and refrigerate until fully chilled, at least 2 hours. Once chilled, divide the mixture among the bowls and top each with a drizzle of olive oil.

Chicken Tortilla Soup

● SERVES 6

I love recipes that turn leftovers into delicious next-day meals, and this soup is one of my favorite ways to turn last night's dinner into a quick dish without sacrificing flavor. In this Mexican soup's traditional form, you'll find golden chicken broth flavored with roasted tomatoes and chilies, then topped with fried tortillas. My version uses similar ingredients, but it has a few time-saving hacks, like using store-bought chicken stock and a can of roasted tomatoes instead of making either from scratch, and I add beans and corn to make it more of a full meal. Note: This recipe includes directions for cooking the chicken from scratch, but if you do use leftover roast chicken, as I often do, you can just shred about 2 cups of it instead.

2 medium skinless, boneless chicken breasts (about 1 pound)

2 tablespoons olive oil

1 large yellow onion, roughly chopped

Kosher salt

4 large garlic cloves, roughly chopped

½ teaspoon dried oregano

1 teaspoon ground cumin

1 teaspoon chili powder

Freshly ground black pepper

1 (14-ounce) can diced fire-roasted tomatoes

4 cups chicken stock

1 (15-ounce) can black beans, drained and rinsed

1 (15-ounce) can corn, drained

Juice of 1 lime

Vegetable oil, for frying the tortillas

4 (6-inch) corn tortillas, cut into ½-inch-wide strips

1 ripe avocado, peeled, pitted, and sliced

¼ cup fresh cilantro leaves

Sour cream and hot sauce for serving (optional)

Lime wedges, for serving

1/ In a medium pot, cover the chicken with cold water by 2 inches. Bring to a boil over high heat, then reduce the heat to medium-low and simmer until the chicken is fully cooked through, 13 to 15 minutes. Remove from the pot with tongs and, once cool enough to handle, shred the meat using two forks. Set aside.

2/ In a large Dutch oven or pot, heat the olive oil over medium heat. When the oil is hot and shimmering, add the onion and a pinch of salt and sauté until the onion is soft and translucent, 5 to 7 minutes. Add the garlic and cook until fragrant, about 1 minute. Add the oregano, cumin, and chili powder, season with salt and pepper, then cook for 1 minute, or until fragrant. Add the tomatoes and stock, increase the heat to medium-high, and bring to a boil, then reduce the heat to medium and cook until slightly reduced, about 15 minutes.

3/ Working in batches, carefully transfer the soup to a high-powered blender, filling it no more than three-quarters of the way, and blend until the soup is completely puréed. (You can also remove the cap from the top of the blender and cover it with a kitchen towel to prevent the lid from popping off.) Transfer to a heatproof bowl and repeat with the remaining soup, then return the puréed soup to the pot. (Alternatively, blend the soup in the pot using an immersion blender.) Add the black beans, corn, lime juice, and shredded chicken and bring to a simmer over low heat while you prepare the tortillas.

4/ Heat ¼ inch of vegetable oil in a medium skillet. After a minute or two, test the oil temperature with a tortilla strip: If it bubbles when a strip is stuck in, then the oil is ready to fry. Add the tortilla strips in batches, making sure not to crowd the skillet, and fry until golden brown, about 2 minutes. Transfer to a paper towel–lined plate and immediately season with salt.

5/ Divide the soup among bowls, then top with the fried tortillas, avocado, and cilantro. Serve immediately with sour cream, hot sauce, if desired, and lime wedges.

Yoni's Strawberry Soup

● **SERVES 4**

Some might argue that strawberry soup is the original smoothie bowl. I will not argue, but in my house, it's known as my brother, Yoni's, soup. End of discussion. Now that that's settled, I'll tell you the story behind it. As a child, I point-blank refused to eat fruit, so when my mom was pregnant with my brother, she actually prayed that he would like fruit. Lo and behold, Yoni has always loved almost every kind of fruit, so at least my parents got one slightly less picky eater.

One thing my mom tried in order to get me to eat more fruit was this strawberry soup. It kind of worked on me, but unsurprisingly, Yoni absolutely LOVED it. The version my mom makes is super simple, so here, I layered in some additional flavors without losing the heart of the soup: its intense strawberry taste. I've paired the soup with a fresh basil oil for an herbal note and also used a tiny bit of cinnamon. I know that a warm spice may seem out of place in an otherwise springy ingredient list, but it's truly the secret ingredient, as the soup doesn't taste like cinnamon at all, but all the ingredients just taste *better*. This soup is a great refreshing lunch on a warm day, with a nice balance between savory and sweet. Smoothie bowl, you've been upgraded!

BASIL OIL

Kosher salt

1 cup tightly packed fresh basil leaves

¼ cup extra-virgin olive oil

STRAWBERRY SOUP

1 (16-ounce) package frozen strawberries

½ cup frozen peaches

¼ cup full-fat plain yogurt

⅓ cup loosely packed fresh basil leaves

3 tablespoons strawberry preserves

Pinch of kosher salt

Pinch of ground cinnamon

1/ MAKE THE BASIL OIL Bring a medium pot of salted water to a boil. While the water comes to a boil, set up an ice bath. Line a fine-mesh sieve with cheesecloth and set it over a medium bowl.

2/ When the water is boiling, add the basil leaves and blanch for 10 to 15 seconds. Using a spider strainer, transfer the basil to the ice bath and swirl the basil leaves around until they're cool enough to handle. Remove them from the ice bath, squeeze as much excess water from the basil leaves as you can, and transfer them to a small food processor. Pulse a few times, then switch to processing on high and stream in the olive oil. Process until the basil leaves are fully puréed with the oil. Pour the mixture into the lined sieve to strain the oil. Discard the solids, transfer the oil to a resealable container, and store in the refrigerator until ready for use. (The oil will last for up to 1 week in the refrigerator.)

3/ MAKE THE SOUP In a high-powered blender, add 14 ounces of the strawberries (about 3 cups), the peaches, yogurt, basil leaves, strawberry preserves, salt, cinnamon, and ½ cup water and blend until the mixture is smooth with a thick, soupy consistency. (If the mixture is too thick, stream in additional water, ¼ cup at a time, until the desired consistency is achieved.)

4/ Dice the reserved 2 ounces strawberries (about ⅓ cup) and set aside for the garnish. (It's okay if they are a little bit frozen.)

5/ Divide the soup among four bowls and garnish with the basil oil and diced strawberries.

And now the chapter you've all been waiting for: Mains, the star of the show! One thing I love about the dishes in this section is that, because most of these recipes make complete meals, they tend to have lots of flavors and textures, and we all know I'm a big fan of both. That also makes them great for sharing with friends and family—the **Braised Lamb with Couscous & Mint Gremolata** on page 173, for instance, is the perfect showstopping labor of love for your next dinner party. And while mains are often centered around an animal protein—you'll find a range of red meat, white meat, and fish here—I also include some equally delicious and hearty vegetarian options, like the **Wild Mushroom Risotto** (page 182) and the **Penne alla Vodka with Burrata** (page 177). Both are perfect when you want something to hunker down with on a cold winter day.

Another fun thing about this chapter is that it will take you around the world more than any other in this book. When I say I learn about cultures through food, this section includes many prime examples! In fact, many of the dishes that follow are the comfort foods of their regions. The **Fish & Chips** (page 185) and **Shepherd's Pie** (page 190) are beloved go-tos all over the United Kingdom, as is the **Chicken Tikka Masala** (page 181) even though its roots are in Indian cuisine. The **Kurdish Shamburak** on page 162 is a treasured Kurdish dish, while **Jeweled Tahdig** (page 174) shows us how much Persian culture values a shared meal through a large pot of delicious rice. So come on in—I'm so excited to show you how I use food to explore the world!

MAINS

Kurdish Shamburak

● MAKES 6 SHAMBURAK

On the corner of a windy street on the side of a hill in the new city of Jerusalem is a restaurant called Ishtabach, which specializes in the Kurdish dish shamburak, the nostalgic comfort-food dish of the owner's childhood. I went to this restaurant on the first night of my first trip to Israel, on the recommendation of my friend and Jerusalem resident Danielle Renov. The restaurant was packed to the gills on a random weeknight evening and buzzing with energy you could feel the moment you walked in the door. I immediately knew from the vibe that whatever I was going to eat would be out of this world.

Shamburak is a thin dough wrapped around a spiced potato mash and flavorful meat filling and shaped like a deliciously stuffed little boat. At Ishtabach, they serve variations with all different kinds of meat, and even vegetarian versions, that are cooked in a huge round clay oven with a rotating tray. After trying several versions with my family, I (of course) became determined to figure out a way to re-create this with a regular stovetop and oven. This recipe features my version of the traditional spiced ground beef topping—I guarantee it will hold you over until you can get to Ishtabach yourself!

DOUGH

1 tablespoon sugar

1 (0.25-ounce) packet active dry yeast

2¼ cups (315g) all-purpose flour, plus more for dusting

1 teaspoon kosher salt

Olive oil, for greasing

POTATO FILLING

4 large russet potatoes (about 2¼ pounds), peeled and cut into small cubes

Kosher salt

2 tablespoons olive oil

1 onion, sliced

2 teaspoons yellow mustard seeds

1 teaspoon ground turmeric

1 teaspoon ground cumin

¼ teaspoon freshly ground black pepper

MEAT FILLING

1 tablespoon olive oil

1 large onion, diced

4 garlic cloves, minced

2 teaspoons ground cumin

1½ teaspoons ground coriander

1 teaspoon cayenne pepper

½ teaspoon ground cinnamon

1 teaspoon kosher salt

1 pound (80/20) ground beef

¼ cup fresh flat-leaf parsley, chopped

Zest and juice of 1 lemon

¼ teaspoon freshly ground black pepper

ASSEMBLY

1 large egg, beaten

Sesame seeds (black or white, or a mix of both), for sprinkling

SERVING

Zhug (spicy cilantro sauce, available in specialty stores and online)

Tahini

Lemon wedges

1/ MAKE THE DOUGH Pour 1 cup room-temperature water into a large bowl, then sprinkle the sugar on top. Add the yeast and whisk lightly to combine. Add the flour and salt and stir with a wooden spoon until all of the dry flour has been absorbed and a shaggy dough forms. Grease a large bowl with olive oil and add the dough, turning to coat all sides with oil. Let rest uncovered for 15 minutes, then perform a series of stretches and folds: wet your hands and pull the edge of the dough up, then fold it over the top of the dough. Work your way around the bowl until a neat ball of dough forms. Repeat this process two more times, then let the dough rest uncovered until doubled in size, about 30 minutes.

2/ MAKE THE POTATO FILLING Add the potatoes to a large pot of cold water and season generously with salt. Bring to a boil over medium-high heat, then reduce the heat to low and simmer until the potatoes are fork-tender, about 12 minutes. Drain the potatoes and set aside. In the same pot, heat the olive oil over medium heat. Add the sliced onion and cook until the edges begin to caramelize, about 8 minutes. Add the mustard seeds, turmeric, cumin, 1 teaspoon salt, and the black pepper. Transfer the cooked potatoes to the pot and mash slightly. Add ½ cup water and stir to combine. Cook for 3 minutes, or until the water is fully absorbed. Set aside to cool slightly, then cover and refrigerate until ready to assemble.

3/ MAKE THE MEAT FILLING In a large frying pan, heat the olive oil over medium heat. Add the onion and garlic and sauté until they begin to caramelize, about 4 minutes. Add the cumin, coriander, cayenne, cinnamon, and salt and cook for 1 more minute, or until fragrant. Add the ground beef and cook for 5 minutes, breaking up the big pieces with a wooden spoon. Remove from the heat, add the parsley and lemon, and stir to combine. Taste and adjust the seasoning with salt and black pepper. Set aside to cool slightly, then cover and refrigerate until ready to assemble.

4/ TO ASSEMBLE Once the dough has doubled, punch it down and divide it into six pieces, about 3 ounces each. Preheat the oven to 500°F and place a baking stone, large skillet, or inverted sheet pan in the oven while it preheats.

5/ On a liberally floured surface, roll each ball of dough into an 8-inch oval about ¼ inch thick. Add ½ cup of the potato mixture to the center, followed by ½ cup of the meat mixture. Form the dough into a boatlike shape, twisting the ends to keep the shape together. Repeat with the remaining dough and filling. Brush the dough of each shamburak with a bit of egg and sprinkle with sesame seeds.

6/ Once all the shamburak have been assembled, open the oven and carefully place the assembled shamburak on the preheated baking stone. (You may need to work in batches, depending on the size of your stone, skillet, or sheet pan.) Bake until golden brown, 8 to 10 minutes. Serve with zhug, tahini, and a fresh squeeze of lemon.

Pizza with Spicy Italian Crumble

When I decided to include a pizza recipe in my book, I knew I had to make it a great one. I'm a big pizza person—I even have a portable, wood-fired pizza oven, and every summer, I invite friends over *at least* once a week for pizza night, when I make pies to order with lots of different topping combinations. That said, I know most people don't have access to a pizza oven, so for this book, I knew I had to find a way to re-create the same effect in a traditional oven.

      The foundation of an exceptional pizza is . . . its foundation: the crust! When pizza goes into a wood-fired oven, the dough at the bottom immediately comes into contact with a screaming hot surface, so the best way to achieve that at home is to bake your pizza in a preheated cast-iron skillet. Cast iron is best because the pan can get incredibly hot and heats evenly, so it mimics the surface of a pizza oven very well—gone are the days of the soggy slice! I also add beer to the dough recipe, because it quickly gives the crust a deep, yeasty flavor that would otherwise require hours and hours of rising time. And finally, to make the crust even more crisp and delicious, I brush it with garlicky olive oil and sprinkle it with salt. Honestly, what's better than pizza with a crust that's basically garlic bread?! This crust is so great that you'll want to use it for ALL toppings, but I've included one of my favorites here, because I like the flavor and texture of a protein crumble, and it makes the pizza more of a complete meal.

PIZZA DOUGH

1 (12-ounce) bottle light beer, at room temperature

1 teaspoon sugar

1 (0.25-ounce) packet active dry yeast

4 cups (560g) all-purpose flour, plus more for dusting

3 tablespoons extra-virgin olive oil, plus more for greasing

2 teaspoons kosher salt

TOPPINGS

1 tablespoon olive oil, plus more for brushing

2 garlic cloves, chopped

8 ounces plant-based protein, crumbled, or hot Italian sausage, casings removed and crumbled

1 teaspoon fennel seeds

¼ teaspoon crushed red pepper flakes

2 tablespoons chopped fresh oregano

2 tablespoons chopped fresh basil leaves

Kosher salt and freshly ground black pepper

½ cup tomato sauce

12 ounces whole-milk mozzarella, shredded

Granulated garlic, for the crust

1/ MAKE THE DOUGH In the bowl of a stand mixer fitted with a dough hook attachment, combine the beer and sugar using a whisk. Sprinkle the yeast on top of the liquid, gently whisk, and allow it to proof for 5 minutes. Once proofed, add the flour, extra-virgin olive oil, and salt. Mix with the dough hook attachment until the dough comes together into a ball. Remove the dough from the mixer and knead on a lightly floured surface until smooth, about 5 minutes.

2/ Place the dough in a large greased bowl, turning it over so the entire surface comes in contact with the oil, then cover with plastic wrap, and set aside in a warm place to rise for 1 hour or until it has doubled in size. Divide the dough into two pieces, transfer them to a sheet pan, and allow them to rise again, loosely covered with plastic wrap, for 30 minutes.

3/ Preheat the oven to 450°F and place a 12-inch cast-iron skillet or baking stone inside while it preheats. (Alternatively, you can use an inverted sheet pan; see Quick Bite.)

4/ MAKE THE TOPPINGS Meanwhile, in a large frying pan, heat 1 tablespoon of the olive oil over medium heat. Add the garlic and cook until fragrant, 1 to 2 minutes. Add your protein of choice and cook until browned, using a wooden spoon to break up the pieces, 3 to 4 minutes for plant-based protein or 6 to 8 minutes for meat-based protein. Season with the fennel seeds, red

pepper flakes, oregano, basil, salt, and black pepper. Cook for an additional minute, then remove from the heat.

5/ Carefully remove the skillet from the oven to a heatproof surface. Working with one piece of dough at a time, stretch it into a 12-inch round, then carefully transfer it to the skillet. Spread ¼ cup of the tomato sauce on top of the dough, leaving a ½-inch border for the edge of the crust. Top with half of the mozzarella, followed by half of the meat crumble. Brush the crust with olive oil, then sprinkle with granulated garlic and salt.

6/ Bake for 15 to 20 minutes, until the crust is golden brown and the cheese is bubbling. Remove from the oven and allow it to cool slightly. Using a flexible heatproof spatula or tongs, remove the cooked pizza from the skillet, then repeat the process with the remaining dough and ingredients, and place it in the oven while you eat the first pizza. Slice the cooked pizza into 6 slices and serve immediately.

QUICK BITE

If you don't have a cast-iron skillet, you can just preheat the oven with a sheet pan placed upside down on the middle rack! It may need a few minutes of extra baking time with this method, so just watch your pizza for bubbly cheese and a crisp, golden crust!

Bulgogi (Korean Grilled Beef)

● **SERVES 4**

Bulgogi is Korean for "fire meat," so unless you're cooking outside, turn on your vent, open your kitchen window, and get ready for some high-heat cooking! Bulgogi has a uniquely delicious flavor thanks to its marinade *and* how that marinade interacts with the high heat that cooks it, since the marinade includes brown sugar and fruit sugar, which both caramelize beautifully. The marinade is packed with other big flavors, like garlic, soy sauce, mirin, and ginger, to name a few. The most distinctive ingredient is puréed Asian pear; it contains an enzyme that helps tenderize the beef, but if you struggle to find one, a regular pear will work, too!

Enjoy bulgogi in a lettuce wrap with steamed white rice, kimchi, green chilies, and thinly sliced scallions. The spice and tang of the toppings complement the sweet, savory beef; the rice acts like a sponge for all the above; and the lettuce gives a fresh, satisfying crunch. Bulgogi is also great as a protein in a rice bowl or in soup, and if you end up eating this by itself, no one will blame you!

1½ pounds well-marbled, boneless sirloin, rib eye, or skirt steak

3 garlic cloves

1 pear, preferably an Asian pear, cut into chunks

½ large onion, cut into chunks

1 (½-inch) piece fresh ginger, peeled and grated

3 tablespoons soy sauce

2 tablespoons dark brown sugar

2 tablespoons mirin (rice wine)

1 tablespoon toasted sesame oil

½ teaspoon freshly ground black pepper

2 tablespoons vegetable oil

Kosher salt

Large lettuce leaves, steamed rice, kimchi, sliced scallions, and green chilies for serving

---

1/ Place the steak in the freezer to firm up for at least 30 minutes while you make the marinade.

2/ In a food processor or high-powered blender, blend the garlic, pear, onion, ginger, soy sauce, brown sugar, mirin, sesame oil, and black pepper until smooth.

3/ Once the steak is firm, thinly slice it against the grain, about ⅛-inch thick. Pour the marinade into a medium bowl, add the beef, and toss to coat. Cover and place in the refrigerator to marinate for at least 1 hour or up to 4 hours.

4/ When ready to cook, heat a large skillet over medium-high heat and add 1 tablespoon of the vegetable oil. Once shimmering, add half of the marinated beef in a single layer, first letting the excess marinade drip off. Sauté undisturbed, until the beef browns and caramelizes, about 2 minutes, then flip and sauté until cooked through and crisp, 2 to 3 minutes more. Transfer to a plate, taste, and season with salt if desired. Repeat with the remaining vegetable oil and beef.

5/ Divide a few lettuce leaves among four plates. Spoon a few tablespoons of rice onto each leaf and top with the bulgogi. Serve with kimchi, scallions, and chilies on the side.

Braised Lamb

WITH COUSCOUS & MINT GREMOLATA

● SERVES 6 TO 8

My brother, Yoni, absolutely loves lamb, so when I want to make him something special, this is my go-to. Ironically, I've never loved lamb myself, but this dish helped me warm up to it. So if this dish converted me, I'm certain it could help *anyone* who's not sure they like lamb yet, either. The lamb shoulder gets super juicy and tender from a slow braising process. It's cooked with orange slices, garlic, shallots, oregano, and rosemary, and when the shredded meat soaks up all those sweet, acidic, herby flavors, the taste is out of this world. To make this a full meal, I like to pile the saucy meat on fluffy couscous, though any pasta or grain would be equally great.

LAMB

2 tablespoons olive oil or vegetable oil

4 to 5 pounds boneless lamb shoulder, fat trimmed, cut into 2-inch pieces

Kosher salt

1 large orange, cut into ¼-inch-thick rounds

1 head garlic, halved crosswise

3 medium shallots, quartered lengthwise

6 pitted Medjool dates, coarsely chopped

2 teaspoons dried oregano

¾ cup dry white wine

1 quart (32 ounces) chicken stock

2 or 3 fresh rosemary sprigs

2 bay leaves

2 tablespoons unsalted butter

Freshly ground black pepper

GREMOLATA

¾ cup fresh mint, coarsely chopped

½ cup fresh dill, coarsely chopped

½ cup fresh flat-leaf parsley, coarsely chopped

½ cup golden raisins

Zest and juice of 1 medium orange

Zest and juice of 1 medium lemon

1 garlic clove, grated

½ cup extra-virgin olive oil

Kosher salt and freshly ground black pepper

Cooked couscous or rice, and yogurt, for serving (I use coconut yogurt)

1/ MAKE THE LAMB Preheat the oven to 325°F.

2/ Heat the oil in a large heavy-bottomed pot or Dutch oven set over medium-high heat. Season the lamb cubes with salt. Working in batches, place the lamb in the pot and sear it on all sides, about 4 minutes per side. Transfer to a plate and repeat with the remaining meat.

3/ In the same pot, add the orange slices and the garlic halves, cut-side down. Cook until slightly charred, about 4 minutes. Flip the orange slices, then add the shallots, dates, and oregano. Stir to combine, making sure the ingredients are well coated in the pan juices, and cook until the shallots are slightly softened, about 4 minutes. Add the wine and cook until reduced by half, about 2 minutes. Add the stock, rosemary sprigs, and bay leaves and bring to a boil. Return the lamb to the pot, and if it is not mostly submerged, add additional water and bring the liquid to a boil. Once boiling, remove the pot from

the heat, cover, transfer to the oven, and braise until the meat is fork-tender and easy to shred, 2 to 2½ hours.

4/ Remove the lamb pieces with tongs and set aside on a plate. Once cool enough to handle, shred the meat.

5/ Strain the braising liquid through a fine-mesh strainer into a bowl and discard the solids. Return the liquid to the pot and bring to a boil over medium-high heat, then reduce the heat to low. Simmer, swirling in the butter until it's melted. Season with salt and pepper. Add the shredded lamb and cook until warmed through, 2 minutes.

6/ MAKE THE GREMOLATA Right before serving, combine all ingredients in a medium bowl, adding salt and pepper to taste, and mix. Serve the lamb over your choice of grain, top with gremolata, and add a dollop of yogurt on the side.

Jeweled Tahdig

● SERVES 4

Literally meaning "bottom of the pot," tahdig is a Persian delicacy, and it gets its name from the layer of rice at the bottom of the pot that browns to crispy, golden perfection. It's traditionally served at weddings, parties, and all kinds of Persian get-togethers. The first time I tried tahdig was at my friend Eitan's house (yes, I have a friend who has the exact same name as me!), and it was made by his Persian grandmother. When it came to the table, I watched his family lovingly fight one another for the crunchy rice, and once I tried it, I was ready to join the competition. The subtle spiced flavor of the fluffy rice contrasts perfectly with the caramelized, crunchy exterior; it's almost like two dishes in one.

Jeweled tahdig is so-called because the bright colors of the pomegranate seeds and chopped pistachios resemble little rubies and emeralds sprinkled on top. My version also has fresh dill for some extra green color and herbaceous flavor. These garnishes not only look beautiful together but also contrast deliciously with the rich saffron-and-yogurt-infused rice.

2 cups basmati rice

1 teaspoon saffron threads

¼ cup hot water

1 tablespoon kosher salt

3 tablespoons vegetable oil or clarified butter

½ teaspoon ground turmeric

¼ cup yogurt, Greek yogurt, or nondairy yogurt

1 large egg yolk

¼ cup pomegranate seeds

2 tablespoons pistachios, chopped

2 tablespoons fresh dill, chopped

½ teaspoon flaky sea salt, for serving

1/ Place the rice in a large bowl and fill it with cold water. Drain, then repeat three more times. Cover with cold water one more time and soak for 30 minutes.

2/ Grind the saffron in a mortar and pestle or in a small bowl using the end of a wooden spoon. Add the hot water and allow it to steep until you are ready to use it.

3/ Bring a large pot of water to a boil. Drain the rice, then add the rice and kosher salt to the pot and cook until a slight bite remains, about 5 minutes. Drain the rice and set aside.

4/ In a medium bowl, whisk together 1 tablespoon of the oil with the turmeric, yogurt, egg yolk, and half of the saffron water (about 2 tablespoons) until well combined. Add in one-third of the cooked rice and stir to coat.

5/ In a large 9- or 10-inch nonstick skillet or pot, heat the remaining 2 tablespoons oil over medium-high heat. Add the rice mixture and spread it out to cover the

bottom of the skillet and about 1 inch up the sides, pressing it down gently with the back of a spatula. Top with the remaining rice and drizzle the rest of the saffron water over the top.

6/ Cook over medium-high heat until you can hear the rice sizzle and the sides of the rice are starting to brown, 4 minutes. Reduce the heat to medium-low and cover, leaving a small gap for steam to escape. Cook for 20 minutes, then turn off the heat. Using a platter that is larger than the skillet, carefully invert the tahdig onto a serving platter. Top with the pomegranate seeds, pistachios, fresh dill, and flaky salt and serve.

QUICK BITE

While I do love this fancy version, you can totally simplify this recipe and use just the rice and saffron. Cook the rice the same way and pour all the saffron water over the rice before cooking.

Penne alla Vodka

WITH BURRATA

● SERVES 4 TO 6

Once it starts getting cold outside, all I want to do is wrap myself up in a big blanket and sit on the couch by a fireplace in cozy PJs watching TV with a huge bowl of this penne alla vodka. My twist on the classic pasta ups the comfort factor by topping the traditional tomato-and-cream-sauce dish with gooey burrata. Trust me: This is hands down the ultimate comfort food. The origin story of this dish is hotly debated—both Italy and the United States claim the invention as their own—but what I know for certain is that this recipe is downright delicious!

Kosher salt

1 pound dried penne pasta

¼ cup olive oil

1 teaspoon crushed red pepper flakes

10 garlic cloves, thinly sliced

3 tablespoons tomato paste

¼ cup vodka

1 (28-ounce) can peeled whole tomatoes in juice, crushed by hand

1 cup heavy cream

1 cup grated Parmesan (30g)

Freshly ground black pepper

1 (8-ounce) ball burrata cheese

Fresh oregano leaves, for garnish

Fresh basil leaves, julienned, for garnish

1/ Bring a large pot of salted water to a boil over high heat. Add the penne and cook, stirring, until just short of al dente (about a minute or 2 less than the cook time on the package), then drain and set aside.

2/ Meanwhile, heat the olive oil in a large saucepan set over medium heat. Add the red pepper flakes and garlic and cook, stirring occasionally, until soft and lightly browned, about 3 minutes. Add the tomato paste and whisk until well combined, then cook for 1 minute. Add the vodka to the pan and let it reduce slightly for about 1 minute. (Or, if you feel up to it, you can flambé the vodka by very carefully lighting the sauce with a long-reach lighter; the flame will go out in 30 to 45 seconds, once the alcohol is cooked off.)

3/ Add the tomatoes and cook, stirring occasionally, until slightly reduced, about 15 minutes. Carefully transfer the sauce to a blender or food processor, working in batches if needed; do not fill it more than three-quarters of the way. Blend until smooth, transfer to a heatproof bowl, then repeat with any remaining

batches. Pour the puréed sauce back into the pan. Stir in the cream and Parmesan, season with salt and black pepper, then stir again until smooth.

4/ Transfer the drained pasta to the pan with the sauce, toss until evenly coated, and transfer it all to a serving platter. Place the burrata in the center of the platter, sprinkle black pepper, oregano, and basil over the top, and serve immediately.

QUICK BITE

Just as the name suggests, the most important ingredient in penne alla vodka is the vodka! Rest assured, all the alcohol is cooked out when you flambé the vodka (fancy-chef lingo for cooking off the alcohol), so this dish is not only delectable but safe for all ages. The vodka plays an essential role in helping the cream and tomato paste emulsify into a perfectly rich sauce, as well as adding a pleasant bite and heat.

Castelvetrano Olive Pesto

WITH CAVATAPPI

● **SERVES 4**

This recipe was inspired by a pair of already great recipes: pesto and tapenade. One of the things I love about pesto is the rich, savory, umami taste from the Parmesan cheese. I wanted to enrich that flavor, so I immediately thought of tapenade and olives.

I didn't want the olives to overwhelm the other pesto flavors, so I went with a Castelvetrano. They're sweet, meaty, and less briny than most olives; their oil also makes the sauce a little more creamy, and they cling to the grooves and curves of the pasta perfectly. For my olive skeptics out there: Please don't let this scare you! Castelvetranos are the gateway olive for the olive hater, and this pesto just tastes richer and—in my opinion—better with them in it.

Kosher salt

1 pound cavatappi or other small, spiral-shaped pasta

1½ cups Castelvetrano olives, pitted

⅓ cup pine nuts, toasted

3 garlic cloves, crushed

3 cups tightly packed fresh basil leaves

¾ cup freshly grated Parmesan cheese

1 cup olive oil

3 tablespoons lemon juice

½ teaspoon crushed red pepper flakes

Freshly ground black pepper

1/ Bring a large pot of heavily salted water to a boil. Add the pasta, cook until al dente according to the package instructions, and drain.

2/ Meanwhile, in a high-powered blender or food processor, pulse together the olives, pine nuts, and garlic until roughly chopped. Add the basil and Parmesan, then blend on low speed while slowly streaming in the olive oil. Taste, add the lemon juice and red pepper flakes, and season with salt and black pepper, then blend until fully combined. Using a spoon, transfer the pesto to a large bowl.

3/ Spoon the pasta on top of the pesto. Stir to fully combine and serve immediately. (Leftovers keep well in an airtight container in the refrigerator for up to 3 days and can also be served cold.)

Chicken Tikka Masala

As a lifelong enthusiast of Indian cuisine, chicken tikka masala was one of the first dishes I fell in love with. The chicken is marinated in a spice-packed mixture similar to traditional Indian chicken tikka kebabs, and then it is wrapped up in a rich, velvety gravy. The succulent chicken is perfect for entertaining and best served with some garlic naan.

● **SERVES 4**

MARINATED CHICKEN

1 (13.5-ounce) can full-fat coconut milk

1 tablespoon grated garlic

1 tablespoon finely grated fresh ginger

1 tablespoon ground turmeric

2 teaspoons garam masala

2 teaspoons ground coriander

2 teaspoons ground cumin

1 teaspoon Kashmiri chili powder (available in specialty stores or online) or regular chili powder

1 teaspoon kosher salt

2 pounds skinless, boneless chicken breasts, cut into 1-inch cubes

Vegetable oil, for greasing

SAUCE

3 tablespoons vegetable oil

6 black cardamom pods

1 teaspoon cumin seeds

1 onion, thinly sliced

1 green chili pepper, such as a Thai green chili or jalapeño, thinly sliced

1 tablespoon finely grated garlic

1 tablespoon finely grated fresh ginger

1 teaspoon ground turmeric

½ teaspoon ground cumin

½ teaspoon Kashmiri chili powder or regular chili powder

½ teaspoon ground coriander

Kosher salt and freshly ground black pepper

¼ cup tomato paste

6 plum tomatoes, puréed (about 2 cups), or 1 (14.5-ounce) can diced tomatoes

1 cup full-fat coconut milk

1 tablespoon fresh lemon juice

Pinch of sugar

¼ cup fresh cilantro, chopped

Garlic Naan (page 52), for serving

1/ MARINATE THE CHICKEN Combine the coconut milk, garlic, ginger, turmeric, garam masala, coriander, cumin, chili powder, and salt in a large bowl. Add the chicken and stir to coat. Cover with plastic wrap and place in the refrigerator for 4 to 6 hours.

2/ When ready to cook, preheat the broiler to high, arrange an oven rack in the top position, and lightly grease a sheet pan. Remove the chicken from the marinade and place it on the prepared sheet pan, reserving the excess marinade. Place on the top rack and broil until it begins to char all around, flipping the chicken halfway through, for 15 to 20 minutes total.

3/ MAKE THE SAUCE In a large pot, heat the oil over medium heat. Add the cardamom pods and cumin seeds and toast for 30 to 45 seconds. Add the onion, chili,

garlic, and ginger. Cook until the onion begins to caramelize around the edges, 7 to 8 minutes. Add the turmeric, ground cumin, chili powder, coriander, and salt and black pepper to taste and sauté for 1 minute. Add the tomato paste and cook until it has darkened, about 3 minutes.

4/ Add the puréed plum tomatoes and bring to a boil over medium-high heat. Reduce the heat to low and simmer, stirring often, until the sauce thickens, 5 minutes. Add the reserved marinade and cook until the mixture is slightly reduced, 10 minutes. Add the cooked chicken, coconut milk, lemon juice, and sugar, then cook until the chicken is opaque, 10 minutes more. Sprinkle the chopped cilantro on top. Serve with garlic naan on the side.

Wild Mushroom Risotto

● SERVES 4

Risotto takes me back to a culinary school intensive I took a few summers ago. There was a whole course dedicated to this Italian classic, a creamy rice dish that is simmered slowly, with warm broth stirred in little by little, so the rice becomes the star of both flavor and texture. Parmesan cheese is folded in at the end *and* grated on top for a nutty, salty finish, and in this version, sautéed mushrooms give the risotto an added boost of umami and savory flavor.

Risotto has a reputation of being complicated, but that's a misconception I want to clear up right now. The actual method isn't hard at all, but it is a dish that requires constant attention (anyone relate?) and continuous stirring (no multitasking please!). Put on your comfiest kitchen shoes, get your stirring arm ready, set your phone to Do Not Disturb, and in about half an hour, you'll have a perfectly creamy result, better than anything you could order in a restaurant!

4 cups vegetable or chicken stock

1¼ sticks (140g) unsalted butter

12 ounces fresh wild mushrooms, wiped clean and sliced

1 large shallot, minced

1 tablespoon fresh thyme, finely chopped

Kosher salt

1¼ cups Arborio rice

⅔ cup dry white wine

⅓ cup freshly grated Parmesan cheese, plus more for serving

¼ cup mascarpone cheese

Freshly ground black pepper

1/ In a medium pot with a lid, bring the stock to a simmer over medium-high heat, then lower the heat to maintain a slow simmer. Cover the pot while you cook the mushrooms.

2/ Melt 1 stick of the butter in a large sauté pan set over medium heat. Add half of the mushrooms and sauté until tender and beginning to brown, 8 to 10 minutes. Using a slotted spoon, transfer the cooked mushrooms to a bowl, leaving the leftover butter in the pan, then repeat with the remaining mushrooms. Set aside.

3/ In the same pan, add the remaining 2 tablespoons butter, the shallot, thyme, and a pinch of salt. Cook until the shallot begins to soften, about 4 minutes. Add the rice and cook for 2 minutes, stirring often, until the edges are translucent and the rice starts to smell nutty. Pour in the white wine to deglaze the pan, stirring it with a spatula and scraping to release any bits that have stuck to the bottom. Simmer, continuously stirring, until the wine has reduced by half, about 1 minute.

4/ Add ¾ cup of the simmering stock and stir occasionally until the rice has absorbed most of the liquid, 2 to 3 minutes, keeping an eye on the pan. Continue adding stock in ¾-cup increments until the rice is al dente and creamy. (You may not need all the stock.) After 25 minutes, start tasting the rice to check its doneness: it should be tender but with a slight bite to it.

5/ Once cooked, remove from the heat and stir in the Parmesan and mascarpone until the cheeses are fully melted and combined with the rice. Add the cooked mushrooms and stir to combine. Season with salt and pepper and garnish with the fresh Parmesan. Serve immediately.

QUICK BITE

Keeping the stock hot while cooking the rice is the key to an exceptional risotto. Slowly adding in the hot liquid over a long period of time is what releases the starches from the rice, which enhances its creamy texture. Risotto is a recipe that requires your full attention over the entire cooking process, but the final product is definitely worth the effort!

Fish & Chips

● **SERVES 4**

Served in paper wrappers everywhere from vendors along the Thames River in London to pubs in the English countryside, fish and chips is arguably the most iconic English dish—and for good reason! The beer-battered fish is deeply golden and crisp on the outside and tender on the inside, and the chips (aka fries) have an extra-soft, pillowy interior and crunchy exterior. This English classic first appeared in the 1860s; interestingly, the tradition of battered and fried fish is believed by some to have been brought over by Jewish immigrants from Spain.

CHIPS

2 pounds red-skinned
    potatoes, peeled and cut
    into ½-inch-thick wedges

Kosher salt

FISH

½ cup plus 2 tablespoons
    all-purpose flour

½ cup cornstarch

1 teaspoon baking powder

Kosher salt and freshly ground
    black pepper

½ cup dark beer, such as Guinness

2 tablespoons vodka

4 (7-ounce) skinless fish fillets,
    preferably sustainable cod,
    pollock, haddock, or another
    thick white fish

TARTAR SAUCE

1 cup mayonnaise

3 tablespoons chopped gherkins

2 tablespoons drained capers,
    roughly chopped

1 tablespoon white wine vinegar

Juice and zest of 1 lemon

2 tablespoons minced shallot

1 tablespoon chopped fresh
    flat-leaf parsley

1 teaspoon kosher salt

½ teaspoon freshly ground
    black pepper

Vegetable oil, for frying
    (about 2 quarts)

Malt vinegar, for serving

1/ MAKE THE CHIPS Fill a large saucepot with water, generously season with salt, and add the potatoes. Bring to a boil over medium-high heat, then reduce the heat to low and simmer for about 10 minutes. Drain the potatoes and place them on a large paper towel–lined sheet pan. Transfer to the refrigerator to cool for at least 30 minutes.

2/ MAKE THE BATTER FOR THE FISH In a large bowl, mix together ½ cup of the flour, the cornstarch, baking powder, ½ teaspoon salt, and ¼ teaspoon pepper. Combine the beer and vodka in a measuring cup. Whisking continuously, add the beer mixture to the flour mixture and continue mixing until you have a thick, smooth batter. Place the batter in the refrigerator uncovered to rest for at least 30 minutes or up to an hour.

3/ MAKE THE TARTAR SAUCE Combine all the ingredients in a medium bowl. Cover and refrigerate to let the flavors develop.

4/ Line two sheet pans with paper towels and place them near the stove. Preheat the oven to 250°F.

5/ In a large pot, heat at least 3 inches of vegetable oil to 350°F. Working in batches, use a spider or slotted spoon to fry potatoes until golden brown, 6 to 7 minutes. Transfer each batch to the prepared pans and season with salt. Place fried potatoes in oven to stay warm.

6/ Pat the fish dry with paper towels and season with salt and pepper. Place remaining 2 tablespoons of flour in a shallow bowl and flour the fish, shaking off excess. Working in batches, dip fish in batter, then use tongs to carefully lower into the hot oil. Fry until golden brown, then remove and drain on prepared pan.

7/ Serve the fish and chips immediately, while hot, with tartar sauce and malt vinegar on the side.

General Tso's Chicken

● **SERVES 4 TO 6**

This Chinese-American dish is beloved by many for its signature sweet and spicy sauce, and I am one of those many. General Tso's has been my go-to Chinese take-out order for as long as I can remember, so—you know where this is going—one day I decided I had to figure out how to make it at home so I could eat it anytime I wanted. This dish combines two of my favorite food properties (fried protein and a complexly flavored sauce), but the ingredients are actually very straightforward. If you are looking to break your take-out habit, this is the go-to.

CHICKEN

Vegetable oil, for frying

½ cup soy sauce

1 large egg

1½ cups cornstarch

2 pounds skinless, boneless chicken breast, cut into 1-inch cubes

SAUCE

2 tablespoons cornstarch

¼ cup sugar

¼ cup soy sauce

1 tablespoon sriracha

¼ cup rice wine vinegar

1 cup chicken stock

1 tablespoon toasted sesame oil

2 large garlic cloves, minced

1 tablespoon minced peeled fresh ginger

1 teaspoon crushed red pepper flakes

1 large scallion, green and white parts sliced, for garnish

White rice, for serving

1/ MAKE THE CHICKEN In a large heavy-bottomed pot, preheat 3 inches of the oil to 350°F. Line a sheet pan with paper towels and set it nearby.

2/ In a large bowl, whisk the soy sauce, ¼ cup water, and egg. Gradually whisk in the cornstarch. It might clump at first, but continue to whisk until the mixture is smooth and uniform; it will also be fairly thick. Add the chicken pieces and mix to fully coat. Working in small batches, use tongs to transfer the coated individual pieces of chicken to the hot oil and cook for 3 to 4 minutes, until golden brown and cooked through. Remove the cooked chicken from the oil and transfer to the prepared sheet pan. Repeat until all the chicken is cooked.

3/ MAKE THE SAUCE In a medium bowl, whisk together the cornstarch, 2 tablespoons water, sugar, soy sauce, sriracha, rice wine vinegar, and chicken stock. Set aside.

4/ In a large wok or sauté pan, heat the sesame oil over medium heat. When the oil is barely smoking, add the garlic, ginger, and red pepper flakes and sauté until fragrant, about 30 seconds. Add the cornstarch mixture and cook, stirring continuously with a wooden spoon, until thickened, 1 to 2 minutes. Add the cooked chicken to the sauce and toss until fully coated. Continue to cook until hot and bubbling, 1 to 2 minutes. Serve in a large bowl topped with sliced scallion and rice.

QUICK BITE

Aside from being a delicious recipe, General Tso's Chicken has a cool science experiment inside of it! If you have ever combined cornstarch and water, then you are familiar with Oobleck. It is a non–Newtonian fluid, which is the technical term for saying that it acts as either a liquid or a solid, depending on the amount of pressure applied to it. While making the chicken's coating, you'll notice that when you slowly mix it, it acts like a liquid, but if you hit the top with a spoon quickly—that is, with more force—it will harden and act like a solid. Try it for yourself and see the magic of Oobleck!

Hummus

WITH SPICED BEEF (HUMMUS BASAR)

● **SERVES 4 TO 6**

Hands down the best way to serve homemade hummus, in my opinion, is Israeli-style, with a heaping pile of sizzling spiced beef (*basar* in Hebrew) on top. The addition of this flavor-packed beef lends rich, savory notes to the hummus and quickly turns—one might say "beefs up"—this snacking dip into a hearty meal for the whole family. This is already a near-perfect combination of taste and texture, but it's even better when heaped on warmed pita bread. To flavor the ground beef, I took inspiration from the meat-topped Syrian flatbread laham bajine, then added tamarind for a tangy note to contrast with the sweet and spicy flavors from the other ingredients.

HUMMUS

2 (15.5-ounce) cans chickpeas, drained but ½ cup chickpea liquid reserved

½ cup olive oil

¼ cup well-stirred premium tahini (I like Seed + Mill)

2 large garlic cloves

Juice of 1 lemon

Kosher salt and freshly ground black pepper

BEEF

2 tablespoons olive oil

1 pound (90/10) ground beef

Kosher salt and freshly ground black pepper

1 medium red onion, sliced (about 2 cups)

8 large garlic cloves, chopped

¼ cup honey

2 tablespoons tamarind paste

1 tablespoon tomato paste

2 teaspoons ground cumin

1 teaspoon smoked paprika

½ teaspoon cayenne pepper

3 tablespoons chopped fresh flat-leaf parsley

¼ cup pine nuts, toasted

Warmed pita bread, for serving

1/ MAKE THE HUMMUS Place the chickpeas and reserved chickpea liquid, olive oil, tahini, garlic, lemon juice, and salt and black pepper to taste in the bowl of a food processor or high-speed blender and blend until smooth, about 5 minutes. Transfer to a bowl, cover, and refrigerate until ready to serve.

2/ PREPARE THE BEEF In a large skillet, heat 1 tablespoon of the olive oil over medium-high heat. Add the ground beef and season with salt and black pepper. Cook until browned, crumbling the meat with the back of a spoon as you go, 6 to 7 minutes. Using a slotted spoon, transfer the beef to a bowl. Pour the remaining 1 tablespoon olive oil into the pan and sauté the onion until it begins to caramelize, 6 to 7 minutes. Add the garlic and cook for an additional minute.

3/ Return the beef back to the skillet and reduce the heat to medium. Add 1 cup water, the honey, tamarind paste, tomato paste, cumin, paprika, cayenne, and salt and black pepper to taste and stir to combine. Cook until most of the liquid has evaporated, 6 to 8 minutes. Add the chopped parsley and pine nuts and mix to combine.

4/ To serve, spoon the hummus onto a large platter or serving bowl, make a well in the center, and pour the beef mixture into the well. Serve with the pita.

QUICK BITE

This recipe will come out great no matter what, but if you do have a little extra time, I highly recommend skinning your chickpeas. Removing the little translucent skin from each bean might not seem like it's worth it, but it's what makes the difference between very good hummus and incredibly delicious, ultra-creamy hummus. (And it's not hard to do: if you hold one between your thumb and index finger, it should pop out of the skin pretty easily.) #FreeThePeas!

Shepherd's Pie

● SERVES 4

A real stick-to-the-ribs meal, shepherd's pie is a classic example of how a mixture of relatively humble ingredients can come together to make one incredible dish. It starts with a super-rich meat-and-vegetable base, flavored with beef stock, red wine, and fresh herbs. You can use lamb or beef in this recipe, but here's a fun fact: If you use beef, you're actually making cottage pie! Shepherd's pie is technically made with lamb (shepherds flock sheep!), but trust me when I tell you that they are equally satisfying.

MEAT FILLING

2 tablespoons olive oil

1½ pounds ground lamb or (80/20) ground beef

1 cup chopped yellow onion

1 cup chopped carrot

2 tablespoons fresh rosemary, chopped

2 tablespoons fresh thyme, chopped

4 garlic cloves, chopped

Kosher salt and freshly ground black pepper

¼ cup tomato paste

2 tablespoons all-purpose flour

1½ cups beef stock

½ cup dry red wine

1 tablespoon Worcestershire sauce

MASHED POTATOES

1½ pounds Yukon gold potatoes (about 3 medium potatoes), peeled and cut into large chunks

Kosher salt

½ cup milk (I use plant-based)

½ stick unsalted butter (I use plant-based)

Freshly ground black pepper

1/ MAKE THE MEAT FILLING Heat the olive oil in a 10-inch cast-iron or oven-safe skillet over medium-high heat. Add the ground lamb and cook for 5 to 7 minutes, breaking it up with a wooden spoon as you go, until cooked through. Remove the meat from the pan with a slotted spoon and set aside. To the same pan, add the onion and carrot and sauté for 4 to 5 minutes, until the edges begin to caramelize.

2/ Stir in the rosemary, thyme, and garlic and cook until fragrant, an additional 2 to 3 minutes. Season with salt and pepper. Add the tomato paste and cook until it begins to caramelize, stirring almost constantly, about 3 minutes. Sprinkle the flour over the top and stir to combine, cooking the flour for 1 minute. Add the beef stock, red wine, and Worcestershire sauce, then deglaze the pan by stirring it with a spatula and scraping to release any bits that have stuck to the bottom. Bring the mixture to a simmer, return the reserved meat to the pan, and stir to combine. Simmer for 5 minutes, or until most of the liquid is cooked out. (If you do not have a cast-iron or oven-safe skillet, transfer the mixture now to a 2-quart baking dish.) Set aside.

3/ MAKE THE MASHED POTATOES Add the potatoes to a large pot and cover with cold water by 1 inch. Generously season the water with salt and bring to a boil over high heat. Reduce the heat to medium-low and cook until the potatoes are fork-tender, 15 to 20 minutes.

4/ Meanwhile, in a small saucepan over medium-low heat, bring the milk and butter to a very gentle simmer.

5/ Preheat the oven to 400°F and place an oven rack in the middle. Drain the cooked potatoes, return them to the pot, and set over medium-low heat for 1 minute to cook off any residual moisture. Remove from the heat, then pass the cooked potatoes through a ricer, or mash them by hand. Whisk half of the warm milk-butter mixture into the potatoes and, once incorporated, add the remaining liquid and whisk again. Season with salt and pepper.

6/ Spoon the mashed potatoes over the meat mixture and spread to the edges to cover. Bake until the top of the mashed potatoes is golden brown on the edges, about 25 minutes.

Israeli-Style Sesame Schnitzel

WITH HERBY TOMATO CUCUMBER SALAD

My favorite thing about schnitzel is that so many different countries have their own version! There's escalope in France, tonkatsu in Japan, Milanese in Italy, chicken-fried steak in the southern United States, and of course, traditional Austrian schnitzel. And that's to name just a few! What makes the Israeli version of this dish distinctive is that the bread-crumb coating contains sesame seeds. Sesame is a common ingredient in Israeli cooking, whether used as whole seeds or ground into tahini. I love them in a schnitzel coating because they add toasty, nutty flavor once they're fried. This meal is one of my family's favorites, so if you're ever over for dinner, there's a pretty good chance I'm serving you sesame schnitzel!

SERVES 4

HERBY TOMATO CUCUMBER SALAD

1 English cucumber, chopped

2 plum tomatoes, seeded and chopped

½ cup chopped red onion

1 garlic clove, chopped

2 tablespoons lemon juice

1 tablespoon olive oil

1 tablespoon chopped fresh dill

1 tablespoon chopped fresh mint

1 tablespoon chopped fresh flat-leaf parsley

Kosher salt and freshly ground black pepper

SESAME SCHNITZEL

4 skinless, boneless chicken breasts

¾ cup all-purpose flour

1 teaspoon kosher salt, plus more as needed

½ teaspoon freshly ground black pepper

2 large eggs

¾ cup panko bread crumbs

¾ cup plain bread crumbs

2 tablespoons white sesame seeds

Vegetable oil, for frying

Ground sumac, for sprinkling

Well-stirred tahini and lemon wedges, for serving

1/ MAKE THE TOMATO CUCUMBER SALAD In a large bowl, combine all the ingredients, adding salt and pepper to taste. Set aside until ready to serve.

2/ MAKE THE SESAME SCHNITZEL Place one of the chicken breasts into a large plastic bag. Pound with the flat side of a meat mallet or rolling pin to ¼-inch thickness. Remove the flattened chicken breast from the bag, set aside, and repeat with the remaining breasts.

3/ Combine the flour, salt, and pepper in a wide bowl. In a separate wide bowl, lightly beat the eggs. In a third wide bowl, mix both the panko and plain bread crumbs, and the sesame seeds. Working with one chicken breast at a time, dredge it in flour so that it is lightly coated all over and tap off any excess. Dip the coated breast into the beaten eggs, letting the extra drip off, then carefully place it in the bowl with the bread crumbs and press

until thoroughly coated on both sides. Set the chicken on a sheet pan and repeat with the remaining breasts.

4/ In a large cast-iron skillet or nonstick pan, heat ½ inch of vegetable oil to 350°F over medium heat. Line a sheet pan with paper towels and set it nearby. Working in batches to not crowd the skillet, carefully place the chicken breasts in the skillet, dropping the chicken, one at a time, away from you to avoid any oil splatters, and fry until golden brown on both sides, 2 to 3 minutes per side. Transfer the cooked chicken to the lined sheet pan and repeat with the remaining chicken. Season to taste with salt and sumac.

5/ Place one schnitzel on each plate and add some of the salad on the side. Drizzle tahini over the top and serve with lemon wedges.

Fennel & Orange Roast Chicken

WITH CREAMY MASHED POTATOES

● SERVES 4

Meat and potatoes! A classic, comforting dinner but also a combination that's been done so many times it's hard to find a new version that's not, well, boring. To combat any potential roast chicken fatigue, I add fennel and orange to this recipe, a fun pairing of flavors that works perfectly alongside a juicy, crispy bird. Roast chickens can often be really dry, but I've *also* solved that problem with a compound butter that goes under the chicken skin and then is spread all over the bird, soaking into the meat while also making the skin deeply golden and crispy. No dry chicken allowed in my house—or yours!

Since the chicken is so flavorful, I like to keep the mashed potatoes pretty mellow. The only major addition is roasted garlic. As the garlic roasts, all the natural sugars caramelize, and the cloves get soft, creamy, and almost sweet. It's a perfect way to enhance the mashed potatoes while still letting the chicken shine.

COMPOUND BUTTER

1 stick salted butter (I use plant-based), softened

2 tablespoons chopped fennel fronds, plus more for serving

Zest of 1 orange (fruit reserved for stuffing the chicken)

1 tablespoon fresh thyme leaves

3 garlic cloves, chopped

Freshly ground black pepper

CHICKEN

2 fennel bulbs, cored and cut into 3-inch-thick wedges, fronds reserved

1 tablespoon olive oil

Kosher salt and freshly ground black pepper

1 (3-pound) whole chicken, giblets removed and discarded, skin patted dry

6 garlic cloves

MASHED POTATOES

1 head garlic

Kosher salt

2 tablespoons olive oil

3 pounds Yukon gold potatoes, peeled and cut into 1-inch cubes

1½ cups milk (I use soy)

1 stick unsalted butter (I use plant-based)

2 fresh thyme sprigs

2 fresh rosemary sprigs

Freshly ground black pepper

PAN SAUCE

1 cup chicken stock

Juice of 1 orange

1/ Preheat the oven to 450°F.

2/ **MAKE THE COMPOUND BUTTER** Combine all the ingredients in a small bowl, adding pepper to taste, and stir until well blended. Set aside.

3/ **PREPARE THE CHICKEN** On a sturdy sheet pan, scatter the fennel, drizzle it with the olive oil, and toss until coated. Season to taste with salt and pepper and set the pan aside.

4/ Place the chicken on a clean work surface and gently separate the skin from the drumsticks, breast, and thighs, using your fingers. Place 2 tablespoons of the compound butter underneath the skin of the first breast and another 2 tablespoons of the compound butter under the skin on the other breast. Flip the chicken over and smear 2 more tablespoons under one thigh and drumstick, and then spread the remaining 2 tablespoons compound butter under the last thigh and drumstick.

recipe continues

5/ Set the chicken on top of the fennel-lined sheet pan, then season the chicken, including the cavities, with salt and pepper. Halve the reserved zested orange and stuff the cavity with the orange halves, garlic, and a few fennel fronds.

6/ Roast for 50 to 60 minutes, or until the internal temperature reaches 165°F. If any portion of the skin becomes too dark, remove the chicken from the oven and gently cover that area with foil. Once cooked through, remove the chicken from the oven, place on a serving platter, and let it rest for 5 to 10 minutes.

7/ PREPARE THE MASHED POTATOES While the chicken is baking, cut off the top of the head of garlic, exposing the top of the cloves. Place the garlic in the middle of a large sheet of tinfoil. Top with a generous sprinkle of salt, drizzle with the olive oil, and securely close the foil. Roast in the oven until golden brown and soft, about 1 hour. Extract the roasted garlic from the bulb by squeezing the bulb gently; discard the bulb. Add the roasted garlic to a bowl and mash with the back of a fork. Set aside.

8/ Add the potatoes to a large saucepot and cover with cold water. Assertively salt the water, bring it to a boil over high heat, then reduce the heat to medium-low and simmer until the potatoes are easily pierced with a paring knife, about 15 minutes. Drain, then return them to the pot over medium-low heat and cook for 1 to 2

minutes, stirring occasionally, to lightly dry the potatoes. Mash the potatoes in the pot with a fork, or grate them on the second largest holes of a box grater.

9/ In a small pot set over medium heat, combine the milk, butter, thyme, and rosemary. Cook until the butter has melted and the flavors have married, 3 to 5 minutes. Discard the herb sprigs.

10/ Slowly drizzle the warm milk mixture over the warm potatoes while mixing with a large whisk. Stir in the mashed roasted garlic, then season to taste with salt and pepper. Cover the potatoes and keep in a warm place until the chicken is ready.

11/ MAKE THE PAN SAUCE While the chicken rests, place the roasted fennel on the serving platter with the chicken and pour off any excess fat that has collected on the sheet pan. Pour the chicken stock and orange juice onto the sheet pan and, using a spatula, gently scrape any browned bits from the bottom of the pan. Carefully place the pan into the oven and reduce the sauce by three-quarters, 5 to 10 minutes. Remove from the oven and pour the sauce through a fine-mesh sieve set over a heatproof bowl.

12/ When ready to serve, carve the chicken and divide the meat among four plates. Serve with the mashed potatoes, pan sauce, roasted fennel, and a garnish of fennel fronds.

I have always had a major sweet tooth. In all honesty, this desserts chapter is really my backup snacks chapter! I could never pick between sweet and savory, but I also don't make it through a single day without something that's mostly sugar and butter, so do with that what you will.

Once you start this chapter, you'll find out that I'm a bit of a dessert snob, so I'll go ahead and break the bad news now: Of course, store-bought or bakery desserts are delicious, and I consume plenty of them myself, but something warm and freshly baked from your home oven can't be beat. If baking intimidates you, don't worry—you'll see how approachable and stress-free it can be. There's even **Five-Ingredient Dulce de Leche Brownies** on page 224 if you need an easy and delicious place to start. And remember: Desserts don't *always* require baking. You can make **Chewy Sea Salt Caramels** (page 214), **Saffron-Cardamom Kulfi** (page 223), and **Cookies & Cream Ice Cream Pie** (page 227) without turning on your oven.

This chapter has something for every craving, from a Jewish bakery classic like the **Babka Two Ways** (page 200) to a rich crème brûlée that's been updated with a version for every season (see page 206). If you like apple pie, I encourage you to try this version with cheddar (page 217). And I've even taken on the ultimate dessert challenge: improving the chocolate chip cookie (page 210). So don't worry—no matter how sweet your sweet tooth is, there's a new favorite dessert in this chapter for you.

DESSERTS

Babka
Two Ways

● MAKES 2 LOAVES OF EITHER
   VARIATION (EACH FILLING RECIPE
   MAKES ENOUGH FOR 2 LOAVES)

Babka is a classic Ashkenazi Jewish dessert, as iconic as matzo ball soup. Its origins date back to nineteenth-century Eastern Europe, when leftover challah dough was rolled with jam or raisins and baked alongside the regular challah loaves. Jewish émigrés brought the dish to the United States, where gooey cinnamon sugar and decadent melty chocolate became more common fillings. I've never been able to choose which one is my favorite between those two, so that's why I've included both filling options in my recipe!

Although cinnamon sugar and chocolate are the most classic of the babka fillings, you can, in fact, fill this timeless treat with pretty much any sort of thick, sweet, delicious spread (including store-bought ones like jam or Nutella if you're short on time), and it'll come out great.

DOUGH

¾ cup (183g) whole milk

1 (0.25-ounce) packet active dry yeast

8 tablespoons (100g) granulated sugar

1 teaspoon kosher salt

3 large eggs, at room temperature

4½ cups (630g) all-purpose flour, plus more as needed

1 stick (110g) unsalted butter, cut into tablespoons, at room temperature, plus more for greasing

CHOCOLATE FILLING (OPTION 1)

10 ounces (283g) semisweet chocolate chips (about 2 cups)

¾ stick (85g) unsalted butter

¾ cup (150g) granulated sugar

½ cup (40g) unsweetened cocoa powder

½ teaspoon pure vanilla extract

CINNAMON FILLING (OPTION 2)

2 cups (400g) packed dark brown sugar

¼ cup (30g) ground cinnamon

1 teaspoon kosher salt

1 stick (110g) unsalted butter, at room temperature

¼ cup (85g) honey

CRUMB TOPPING

½ cup (70g) all-purpose flour

½ cup (100g) granulated sugar

¼ cup (53g) vegetable oil

½ teaspoon pure vanilla extract

Pinch of salt

1 large egg, beaten, for egg wash

1/ MAKE THE DOUGH In a small saucepan set over low heat, heat the milk until it is warm to the touch. (It should be about 105°F, but no warmer than 110°F.) Pour the warmed milk into the bowl of a stand mixer fitted with the dough hook attachment and sprinkle the yeast and 1 tablespoon of the granulated sugar over. Let sit until foamy, about 5 minutes.

2/ After it blooms, add the remaining 7 tablespoons granulated sugar, the salt, eggs, and flour to the milk mixture. Start mixing on low speed, then gradually raise the speed to medium and mix until the ingredients are fully combined. Increase the speed to medium-high and knead for an additional 5 minutes. The dough will look

very sticky but should form a ball around the dough hook. After 5 minutes, slowly add the butter, 1 tablespoon at a time, fully incorporating it into the dough before adding the next tablespoon. Once all the butter has been added, knead for an additional 5 minutes, or until the dough pulls away from the sides of the bowl. (If the dough looks sticky, add additional flour, 1 tablespoon at a time, until the dough is smooth and shiny.) Once the dough has pulled away from the bowl, knead for an additional 5 minutes on medium speed. Transfer the dough to a bowl greased with butter, cover, and let rise in a warm place until doubled in size, 1 to 1½ hours.

recipe continues

3/ MAKE YOUR FILLING OF CHOICE If making the chocolate filling, set up a double boiler by bringing a few inches of water to simmer in a small saucepan, then place a heatproof metal or glass bowl directly on top of the saucepan. (Make sure the water is not touching the bottom of the bowl.) Add the chocolate chips and butter and stir until fully melted. Add the granulated sugar, cocoa, and vanilla and stir until fully combined. Remove from the heat. If making the cinnamon filling, in a small bowl, mix together the brown sugar, cinnamon, and salt, then set aside.

4/ MAKE THE CRUMB TOPPING In a small bowl, combine the flour, granulated sugar, oil, vanilla, and salt with a fork until it has a crumb-like consistency. Place in the refrigerator until ready to use.

5/ Grease two 5 × 9-inch loaf pans.

6/ Punch down the dough, then divide it in half. Place one dough ball in the refrigerator, covered, until ready to use.

7/ On a clean surface and using a rolling pin, roll out the first dough ball into a rectangle about 12 inches wide, at least 24 inches long, and no thicker than ¼ inch. You should not need any additional flour for rolling, but if your dough is sticking or tearing, lightly flour your surface and rolling pin.

8/ If you're using the chocolate filling, gently spread half of it on each rectangle, being careful not to tear the dough. Starting on one long side, roll into a tight log and refrigerate. Repeat with second half of dough.

9/ If using the cinnamon filling, spread the butter evenly on both rectangles, saving a little border on the long side. Sprinkle half the sugar mixture on top, then drizzle half the honey over the sugar. Starting on one long side, roll into a tight log and refrigerate. Repeat with second half of dough.

10/ Place both logs vertically on your work surface, crossing the top of one over the other, and pinch the tops together with your fingers. Twist the logs to form one long coil, then fold the coil in half so that one half of the coil sits on top of the other. Twist these two layers together once, or twice if possible. If your folded coil seems very short, gently pull and stretch the dough until it's about 14 inches long. Cut this log in half crosswise, and place each half in a prepared loaf pan.

11/ Cover the pans with a clean kitchen towel and let rise in a warm, draft-free spot until the babka has filled out the pans, 30 to 40 minutes.

12/ While the babka rises again, preheat the oven to 350°F.

13/ After the second rise, brush the top of the dough with the beaten egg wash, then divide the crumb filling and sprinkle half on top of each loaf. Bake until golden brown, 35 to 40 minutes.

14/ Remove the babkas from the oven and let them cool on a wire rack for 20 minutes, or until the loaf pans are easier to handle. Carefully tip each loaf out onto a cooling rack. Slice and enjoy warm!

Pistachio Baklava

● MAKES 20 PIECES

While walking through Mahane Yehuda Market in Jerusalem with my family on my first trip to Israel, it was impossible to miss the intoxicating smell that came from the stands selling sweets. Even though I had tried baklava many times before, there was something about the smell of the baklava in the Shuk (as the market is known) that made my mouth water. About three seconds after my first bite, I was determined to re-create a version as close to that one as possible back in my home kitchen.

Baklava is a Middle Eastern delicacy made of layers of paper-thin phyllo dough that gets brushed with melted butter, filled with chopped nuts, and then is covered in a sticky and sugary syrup when it's hot from the oven. It'll be hard to wait for it to cool before you eat it, but as a person who's burned their mouth while sneaking a piece too soon, trust me when I tell you it's very much worth the wait!

3½ sticks (385g) unsalted butter

4 cups (560g) unsalted pistachio nuts, finely chopped

1 cup (200g) sugar

3 teaspoons ground cinnamon

1 (16-ounce) package phyllo dough, thawed

1 cup (340g) honey

1 teaspoon kosher salt

1 tablespoon freshly squeezed lemon juice

1/ Preheat the oven to 350°F and place a rack in the center.

2/ Melt 2 sticks of the butter in a small saucepan set over medium-low heat. In a medium bowl, combine the pistachios, melted butter, ⅔ cup of the sugar, and 2 teaspoons of the cinnamon.

3/ Melt the remaining 1½ sticks butter in a small saucepan over medium-low heat. Place the stack of phyllo sheets on a clean work surface. Cover with a layer of plastic wrap, then place a damp kitchen towel over top.

4/ Brush a 9 × 13-inch baking dish with a thin layer of the melted butter. Trim the stack of phyllo sheets with a sharp knife or pair of scissors so that the width and length are the same as your baking dish. Place 2 sheets of phyllo in the baking dish. Brush the top layer with butter, then top with another 2 sheets. Repeat the process until you have four layers of buttered phyllo.

5/ Pour half of the pistachio mixture on top of the phyllo. Top with 2 more sheets of phyllo and repeat the layering process with six more layers of phyllo. Pour the remaining half of the pistachio mixture on top, then add 2 more sheets of phyllo dough. Repeat the butter-layering process with six more layers of phyllo. Brush the top layer with butter.

6/ Using a sharp knife, cut the baklava on an angle into 1½-inch diamonds. Bake until golden brown, rotating the baking dish halfway through, 40 to 45 minutes.

7/ While the baklava is in the oven, combine the remaining ⅓ cup sugar and 1 teaspoon cinnamon, the honey, salt, lemon juice, and 2 tablespoons water in a small saucepan. Bring to a boil over medium heat, making sure the sugar is completely dissolved. Reduce the heat to low and allow the mixture to simmer for 5 minutes. Remove from the heat and let cool.

8/ When the baklava is finished cooking, drizzle the syrup immediately over the top. For best results, allow the baklava to cool to room temperature, then cover with tinfoil and rest overnight before eating. (Though if you are short on time or super impatient like I am, you can eat it right after it cools down!)

Crème Brûlée for Every Season

● MAKES 6 CUSTARDS

Like many people, I fell for crème brûlée at a fancy restaurant. At first, it seemed like something too intimidating to make at home, but I discovered that it's actually a fairly simple recipe with just four basic ingredients—cream, vanilla, eggs, and sugar. Anyone, with any level of culinary ability, can master it with a few essential tips.

Since I feel strongly that this is a dessert you should be able to have any time of the year, I created four different flavors, one for each season. No matter which month it is, I guarantee that your guests will be awed when you offer them each a homemade crème brûlée at the end of the meal. Whether or not you tell them how ridiculously easy it is to make is totally up to you—my lips are sealed!

SEASONAL FILLING OF CHOICE

SPRING

¾ cup Rhubarb Jam (recipe follows)

SUMMER

¾ cup Blueberry-Thyme Jam (page 51)

FALL

¾ cup Chocolate Fudge Sauce (page 227)

WINTER

¾ cup Grapefruit Curd (recipe follows)

2 cups (470g) heavy cream

1 vanilla bean, split lengthwise, seeds scraped, or 1 teaspoon pure vanilla extract or vanilla paste

4 large egg yolks

½ cup sugar (100g), plus more for topping

1/ Preheat the oven to 325°F.

2/ Add 2 tablespoons of the seasonal filling of your choice to the bottom of six ramekins and place them in the freezer to firm up.

3/ In a small pot over medium heat, bring the cream and vanilla to a simmer. Reduce the heat to low and simmer for 2 to 3 minutes. Remove from the heat and let cool. Remove the vanilla bean (if used).

4/ While the cream cools, in a large bowl, whisk the yolks and sugar together until the mixture is thickened and pale yellow. (This is called "ribbon stage.") To test, lift the whisk about an inch over the mixture and, using what drips off the whisk, draw an S shape on the mixture; once the S holds for 2 to 3 seconds before dissolving, it's ready. Pour a quarter of the cream into the egg mixture and immediately whisk vigorously until combined. Slowly stream in the remaining cream and whisk until thoroughly combined.

5/ Set a kettle of water to boil. Remove the ramekins from the freezer, divide the custard evenly among them, and place them in a 9 x 13-inch baking dish. Carefully pour boiling water into the baking dish halfway up the sides of the ramekins. Place in the oven and bake until the centers are barely set, 35 to 40 minutes. Remove the ramekins from the baking dish and let cool at room temperature for 15 minutes, then cover with plastic wrap and refrigerate for at least 3 hours or up to 2 days.

6/ To serve, sprinkle each ramekin with a heaping teaspoon of sugar in an even, thin layer and place the ramekins on a sheet pan. Place the ramekins on the top rack under a broiler, or hold a handheld cooking torch a few inches from the surface, and broil until all the sugar melts and begins to turn golden brown and caramelized. (If you're using a broiler, keep a very close eye on the sugar; it will take between 1 and 3 minutes, but it can burn quickly!) Serve within an hour of caramelizing.

Rhubarb Jam

4 ounces (113g) rhubarb, ends trimmed and cut into ½-inch pieces (about 2 cups)

¾ cup (150g) sugar

1/ In a medium saucepan set over medium-high heat, combine the rhubarb and sugar. Cook, stirring occasionally, until the rhubarb releases its juices and the mixture comes to a boil, 5 to 7 minutes. Reduce the heat to medium and cook, stirring often, until the foam subsides and the jam is thickened, 10 to 15 minutes.

2/ Transfer the mixture to a heatproof container and let cool to room temperature. Cover and place in the refrigerator for at least 1 hour before using. (Leftovers can be stored in an airtight container in the refrigerator for up to 1 month.)

Grapefruit Curd

4 large egg yolks, at room temperature

½ cup (100g) sugar

Juice of ½ grapefruit plus 1 teaspoon zest

¾ stick (83g) unsalted butter, cut into tablespoons, at room temperature

Set up a double boiler by bringing a few inches of water to a simmer in a small saucepan, then place a heatproof metal or glass bowl directly on top of the saucepan. (Make sure the water is not touching the bottom of the bowl.) Add the egg yolks, sugar, and grapefruit juice to the bowl and whisk until smooth. Continue whisking vigorously and constantly for 20 to 25 minutes, until the mixture looks thick. Remove from the heat and stir in the butter, 1 tablespoon at a time, until well combined. Strain through a fine-mesh strainer, discard the solids, and stir in the grapefruit zest. Let cool to room temperature, then cover with plastic wrap or transfer to a container with a tight-fitting lid and place in the refrigerator for at least 1 hour before using. (Leftovers can be stored in an airtight container in the refrigerator for up to 1 month.)

Chocolate Chunk Cookies

WITH BROWN BUTTER AND BOURBON

My favorite food in the ENTIRE world is a chocolate chip cookie! (Except on the days when it's a cinnamon roll; see page 23.) So, of course, I am also a proud chocolate chip cookie snob. When I say they're my favorite food, what I mean is I want every single element of the cookie to be the very best: The butter is browned, the chocolate is semisweet and chopped by hand, and there's flaky sea salt (and bourbon), too. These are your childhood chocolate chip cookies all grown up, and I proclaim them The Best Chocolate Chunk Cookie!

● **MAKES 16 COOKIES**

2 sticks (220g) unsalted butter

1¼ cups (250g) packed dark brown sugar

¼ cup (50g) granulated sugar

1 large egg

1 large egg yolk

1 tablespoon bourbon

2 teaspoons pure vanilla extract

1¾ cups (245g) all-purpose flour

¾ teaspoon baking soda

1 teaspoon kosher salt

8 ounces (227g) semisweet chocolate, chopped into small chunks (about 2 cups)

Flaky sea salt

1/ Place the butter in a medium saucepan (preferably with a light-colored interior, so you can monitor the browning) set over medium-low heat. Melt the butter and cook, swirling occasionally. The butter will foam and begin to change color, from yellow to amber. Continue cooking and swirling the pan, until the milk solids separate and begin to brown. Once the milk solids are a caramel color and smell nutty (anywhere from 5 to 8 minutes, depending on the pan), immediately remove it from the heat. Pour it into a heat-safe bowl and set in the refrigerator to cool for 15 minutes.

2/ In the bowl of a stand mixer fitted with the paddle attachment, cream the cooled brown butter, brown sugar, and granulated sugar on medium speed for 3 to 4 minutes. (The mixture will lighten in color a bit, but it will not be as fluffy or pale as regular creamed butter.) Scrape down the sides of the bowl, then add the egg, egg yolk, bourbon, and vanilla and beat for 1 to 2 minutes, until the ingredients are thoroughly creamed together.

3/ Scrape down the sides of the bowl again, add the flour, baking soda, and kosher salt, and mix at the lowest speed until just a few streaks of flour remain. Stir in the chocolate chunks until just combined. Using a

2-tablespoon cookie scoop or spoon, portion the dough onto a parchment-lined sheet pan, then place in the freezer for 20 minutes.

4/ While the dough is in the freezer, preheat the oven to 350°F and line two sheet pans with parchment paper. Position the oven racks in the upper and lower third of the oven. After 20 minutes, place the cold dough balls on the prepared sheet pans, leaving about 4 inches between each cookie, or about 6 cookies per sheet pan.

5/ Place the sheet pans in the oven and bake for 12 minutes, or until the cookies turn a golden brown color on the edges, rotating the pans halfway through. Remove the cookies from the oven and let cool on the sheet pans for 2 minutes, then transfer to a cooling rack. Sprinkle with flaky salt while still warm. Repeat with the remaining dough.

QUICK BITE

Freezing the dough may seem like an odd step, but it serves two important functions: It keeps the cookies from spreading too thin as they cook (I like a thick, barely-cooked-in-the-center cookie!), and it flash-freezes the dough (in case you want to bake the cookies in batches).

Chocolate Tahini Cake

WITH TAHINI & HALVA CRUMB TOPPING

If you've made it this far in my book, you may have noticed that I LOVE tahini! You might also have realized that cake has never been my favorite dessert. So I knew that if I was going to put a cake in my book, it would have to be filled with things I love. You already know there's tahini, but there's also a crumb topping that's chock-full of halva (see Quick Bite). This cake is super moist as if your favorite boxed cake mix got a major upgrade.

● **MAKES ONE 8-INCH ROUND CAKE**

CRUMBLE

¾ cup (105g) all-purpose flour

½ cup (50g) firmly packed light brown sugar

1 teaspoon ground cinnamon

½ teaspoon kosher salt

½ stick (55g) cold unsalted butter, cut into cubes

2 tablespoons well-stirred tahini

1 teaspoon pure vanilla extract

½ cup crumbled halva (see Quick Bite)

CAKE

Nonstick cooking spray

1½ cups (210g) all-purpose flour

½ cup (40g) unsweetened cocoa powder

½ teaspoon baking powder

½ teaspoon kosher salt

½ teaspoon baking soda

¾ cup (150g) granulated sugar

2 large eggs, at room temperature

¼ cup (60g) whole milk

¼ cup (60g) sour cream

½ cup (105g) vegetable oil

¼ cup (70g) well-stirred tahini

1 teaspoon pure vanilla extract

½ cup (118g) boiling water

SERVING (OPTIONAL)

½ cup chopped dark chocolate

1 tablespoon sesame seeds

1/ MAKE THE CRUMBLE Combine the flour, brown sugar, cinnamon, and salt in a medium bowl. Mix until well blended. Add the butter and, using your clean fingers, work the butter into the flour mixture until large clumps form. Add the tahini and vanilla and stir with a spoon until incorporated. Add the crumbled halva, stirring to combine, and set aside in the refrigerator.

2/ MAKE THE CAKE Preheat the oven to 350°F. Line an 8-inch springform pan with parchment paper and coat it with cooking spray.

3/ In a large bowl, sift together the flour, cocoa powder, baking powder, salt, and baking soda. Add the granulated sugar and whisk until well combined.

4/ In a separate medium bowl, whisk together the eggs, milk, sour cream, vegetable oil, tahini, and vanilla. Add the wet ingredients to the dry ones and whisk until blended and no streaks of flour remain. Whisk in the boiling water, stirring until smooth.

5/ Scrape the batter into the pan, smooth the top, and bake for 20 minutes. Scatter the crumble on top of the cake and bake until a cake tester inserted in the center comes out clean, an additional 20 to 25 minutes.

6/ Let the cake cool for at least 30 minutes, then remove it from the pan. If you're making the melted chocolate, 5 to 10 minutes before serving, place the chopped chocolate in a microwave-safe bowl and microwave on high in 30-second intervals, stirring in between, until the chocolate is fully melted. Drizzle the chocolate over the top and sprinkle with sesame seeds before serving, if desired.

QUICK BITE

Halva is an extremely delicious, sweet nutty candy found all over the Middle East. There are countless regional variations, but one of the most common is made from . . . wait for it . . . sesame seeds. (Just like tahini!) It's available at specialty groceries or online from companies such as Seed + Mill.

Chewy Sea Salt Caramels

● **MAKES 64 CARAMELS**

There is just something utterly irresistible about a sea salt caramel. It's perfectly soft and chewy, creamy and sweet, and barely bitter; and with a generous sprinkle of flaky sea salt, the result is a not-too-sweet treat. When sugar, corn syrup, butter, cream, and vanilla are boiled to the right temperature, something truly magical happens. This candy's petite size makes it perfect for satisfying all your sweet cravings in a single bite.

I know that making candy at home might seem intimidating, but as long as you have a thermometer (or use the method described in Quick Bite to get to the correct consistency), these caramels can be cooling in your kitchen after just twenty minutes. One batch makes more than sixty individual caramels, so give them away to friends, or keep your candy dish stocked with something homemade! I've heard they'll last for weeks in an airtight container in the refrigerator, but for some reason they've never lasted that long in my house. . . .

Nonstick cooking spray

1 cup (200g) packed dark brown sugar

½ cup (100g) granulated sugar

½ cup (170g) light corn syrup

1 cup (235g) heavy cream

1 stick (110g) unsalted butter, cut into several slices

1 teaspoon pure vanilla extract

¼ teaspoon kosher salt

1 teaspoon flaky sea salt

1/ Line an 8 × 8-inch baking pan with parchment paper, leaving a little bit of overhang around the sides, then coat it with nonstick cooking spray. Set aside.

2/ In a medium heavy-bottomed pot, bring the brown sugar, granulated sugar, and corn syrup to a boil over medium heat, swirling the pan as it cooks to ensure the ingredients are well incorporated. Once the sugar mixture is boiling and the sugar has dissolved, carefully add the heavy cream and butter, then stir gently. Continue cooking, undisturbed, until a candy thermometer or instant-read thermometer registers 255°F, or the mixture has reached the "hard ball" stage (see Quick Bite). Immediately remove the pot from the heat and stir in the vanilla and kosher salt.

3/ Pour the mixture into the prepared baking pan and top with the flaky salt. Place the pan in the refrigerator to chill until firm, about 2 hours. Once firm, remove the caramel sheet from the pan by lifting out the parchment paper and transfer it to a cutting board. Cut into small squares and wrap each in a piece of wax or parchment paper, if desired.

QUICK BITE

If you don't have a candy thermometer, you can use a bowl of ice water to test the temperature. While the candy is cooking, periodically drop a small spoonful of the candy into the bowl of ice water. Place your hand in the water, attempt to form the sugar into a ball, and bring it out of the water. The shape and texture of the resulting sugar ball will tell you the approximate temperature of your candy. Once the caramel holds itself together and is soft and malleable, similar to the consistency of a soft caramel, that means it's reached the hard ball stage and is ready to be poured into the prepared baking pan.

Cheddar Apple Pie

● **MAKES ONE 9-INCH PIE**

Yes, you read that right: This New England classic gets showered in super-sharp cheddar CHEESE! Think of how fruit is usually served on a cheese board, or how apples and cheese are both delicious additions to a salad. The cheese is creamy, salty, and savory, whereas the apple is tart, crisp, and sweet. I promise the addition of cheddar cheese elevates the flavor in a subtle, but very delicious way.

If you're not sold on this combination of flavors just yet, know that the cheese also helps give this pie a super-tender, flaky crust. Usually, the little bits of cold butter fat in the dough are what create those flaky layers in the oven, but in this crust, you also have the fat from the grated cheddar!

DOUGH

3 cups (420g) all-purpose flour, plus more for dusting

1 teaspoon kosher salt

2 tablespoons granulated sugar

2 sticks (220g) cold unsalted butter, cut into ½-inch cubes

1½ cups (150g) grated aged cheddar, plus more for sprinkling

⅔ cup (157g) ice water

FILLING AND ASSEMBLY

4 pounds Pink Lady apples, peeled, cored, and sliced ⅛ inch thick

2 tablespoons freshly squeezed lemon juice

¾ cup (150g) well-packed dark brown sugar

2 teaspoons ground cinnamon

1 teaspoon kosher salt

½ stick (55g) unsalted butter

⅓ cup (47g) all-purpose flour

1 egg, lightly beaten, for egg wash

1/ MAKE THE DOUGH In a large bowl, mix the flour, salt, and granulated sugar. Using a pastry cutter or your clean fingers, cut the butter into the flour mixture until the texture resembles coarse cornmeal and the butter pieces are no larger than small peas. Add the cheddar and mix until evenly distributed and coated in flour. Slowly pour in the ice water, 1 tablespoon at a time, and using clean hands, mix just until it starts to come together. Dump the dough out onto a clean, lightly floured work surface. Form the dough into a rough ball with your hands until it is mostly combined. (If the dough is very sticky, place it in the freezer for 5 minutes.) Divide the dough in half and form two disks. Wrap each disk in plastic wrap and refrigerate for at least 1 hour.

2/ Remove one of the disks of dough from the refrigerator. On a lightly floured surface, roll the dough into a 12-inch round that is ⅛ inch thick. Place the sheet of pie dough into a 9-inch pie plate. Leaving about 1 inch of overhang, cut the excess dough from the edges and place the pie plate in the refrigerator to chill while preparing the filling.

3/ MAKE THE FILLING Combine the apples, lemon juice, brown sugar, cinnamon, and salt in a large bowl, tossing gently. Allow the mixture to macerate for 10 minutes, then pour the excess liquid into a small bowl and reserve. Set the apples aside.

4/ In a small saucepot over medium heat, melt the butter. Sprinkle the flour over the butter and whisk to combine. Cook until the mixture turns dark blond and smells nutty, whisking frequently, 2 to 3 minutes. Add the reserved apple liquid and bring to a simmer. Simmer for 1 minute, or until the mixture has thickened to resemble a thick caramel sauce. Pour over the reserved apples and toss to combine.

recipe continues

5/ TO ASSEMBLE Remove the pie plate from the refrigerator, then pour the apple mixture into the crust. Using the back of a spoon, flatten the apples so they are flush with the top of the pie plate. Return to the refrigerator to chill.

6/ On a lightly floured surface, roll out the remaining round of dough into a 12-inch circle that is ⅛ inch thick and cut it into ten 1-inch-wide strips. Remove the pie from the refrigerator and lay five of the dough strips evenly spaced across the top. Weave the other five dough strips perpendicularly through the previous strips to make a lattice or basket-weave design across the entire pie. Trim the excess dough from the edges of the plate. Pinch the bottom-crust edge and lattice edge together and lightly roll the pinched crust underneath itself. Brush the surface of the dough with the beaten egg and sprinkle with finely grated cheddar. Refrigerate for at least 30 minutes before baking.

7/ While the pie is chilling, preheat the oven to 425°F.

8/ Place the pie on a rimmed sheet pan and bake for 25 to 30 minutes, then reduce the oven temperature to 350°F and bake for an additional 30 minutes, or until the crust is golden brown and you can see the filling bubbling between the lattice strips. (If the crust browns too quickly, remove it from the oven and tent tinfoil over any darker areas.) Remove the pie from the oven and let cool at least 2 hours before serving.

QUICK BITE

The star of the show—the apples—end up perfectly cooked, thanks to some maceration time before they're baked. Then those extra juices are thickened with butter and flour before going into the pie shell, so you'll find no mushy fruit or soggy bottom crust here. It's a foolproof filling method that will win you over after just one bite!

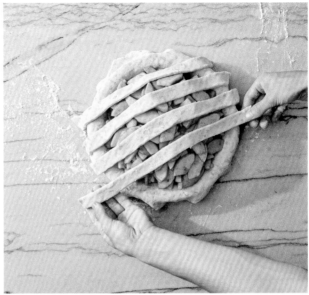

Blueberry Cardamom Hand Pies

A few summers ago, I went blueberry picking with my family in Connecticut. If you've ever gone fruit picking, you probably know what I'm going to say next: We came home with way more blueberries than we could ever possibly eat! My mom challenged me to come up with a creative way to use them before they spoiled. I've always loved cardamom, and we had a trunk full of blueberries, and thus the beginnings of this recipe were born!

● MAKES 9 HAND PIES

DOUGH

3 cups (420g) all-purpose flour, plus more for dusting

1 tablespoon granulated sugar

1½ teaspoons kosher salt

2 sticks (220g) cold unsalted butter, cut into ½-inch cubes

1 large egg, beaten

⅓ cup (79g) ice water

FILLING

2 cups (280g) blueberries

¼ cup (50g) granulated sugar

1 tablespoon all-purpose flour

1 tablespoon lemon juice

¼ teaspoon ground cardamom

½ teaspoon kosher salt

ASSEMBLY

1 egg, lightly beaten, for egg wash

2 tablespoons dark brown sugar or demerara sugar

1/ MAKE THE DOUGH In a large bowl, combine the flour, sugar, and salt. Using a pastry cutter or your fingers, cut in the butter until the texture resembles coarse cornmeal. Pour in the egg and ice water and gently mix with a fork until a shaggy dough forms.

2/ Pour the dough onto a lightly floured work surface and gently pat it into a rectangle. Fold it in half, then pat it into a rectangle again. Repeat these steps twice more to create layers in the dough, then divide the dough in half (each half should be a square) and wrap each half tightly in plastic wrap. Place in the refrigerator and let rest for at least 1 hour or up to 2 days.

3/ MAKE THE FILLING In a medium saucepan set over medium heat, stir together the blueberries, sugar, flour, lemon juice, and cardamom and bring the mixture to a simmer. Cook until the sugar has fully dissolved, the mixture has thickened, and the blueberries have begun to burst, about 5 minutes. Remove the saucepan from the heat, stir in the salt, and let cool.

4/ Line a sheet pan with parchment and set aside.

5/ Remove one square of dough from the refrigerator. On a lightly floured surface, roll it out to a 9 × 9-inch square about ¼ inch thick. If the edges of the dough crack, let it sit at room temperature for 10 to 15 minutes to warm up slightly. Using a pizza cutter or chef's knife, cut the dough into nine 3 × 3-inch squares. Place the squares on the lined sheet pan, top each with a heaping tablespoon of blueberry filling, and place in the refrigerator.

6/ Remove the second square of dough from the refrigerator and, on a lightly floured surface, roll it out into a slightly larger square, about 10 × 10 inches. Cut this piece of dough into 9 equal squares and cut a small X into the center of each square to serve as a vent. Remove the filled pie bases from the refrigerator and brush some of the egg wash around the perimeter of each square. Place one piece of vented dough on top of each base and crimp the edges together using a fork. Brush the tops with the egg wash, sprinkle with the brown sugar, and return to the refrigerator for 10 minutes to chill once more before baking.

7/ Preheat the oven to 400°F. Bake the pies until deeply golden brown, 25 to 30 minutes. Let the pies cool on the sheet pan for 10 minutes, then transfer to a wire rack to cool completely.

Saffron-Cardamom Kulfi

● MAKES 8 KULFI

Sold by vendors along the streets of India and at Indian restaurants around the world, kulfi is a sweet frozen treat. Traditionally, it is prepared by cooking sweetened milk over low heat for many hours until it reduces and thickens. Often, when making kulfi at home, heavy cream and sweetened condensed milk are used to speed up the process. The semi-condensed mix is then flavored and frozen Popsicle-style in cone-shaped molds with a lid. Some of the classic flavors are malai (cream), rose, mango, cardamom, saffron, and pistachio.

I have loved kulfi ever since the first time I had it at an Indian restaurant in Manhattan. After *many* failed attempts to re-create my favorite Indian sweet, I finally nailed it one day when I had a lot of leftover heavy cream and sweetened condensed milk that I needed to use. After playing around with a few different methods and ratios of ingredients, I finally arrived at this one, which gave my kulfi that signature dense, custardy texture. The final result was an out-of-this-world frozen treat with a mouthwatering flavor profile from spices and nuts that makes regular ice cream seem literally vanilla by comparison.

4 cups heavy cream

1 (14-ounce) can sweetened condensed milk

3 tablespoons sugar

6 whole green cardamom pods

1 teaspoon ground cardamom

¼ teaspoon saffron threads

¼ cup finely chopped pistachios

SPECIAL EQUIPMENT

Kulfi or ice pop molds (optional)

1/ In a medium pot, bring the heavy cream to a simmer over medium heat. Pour in the condensed milk, sugar, cardamom pods, ground cardamom, and saffron. Once the mixture comes to a boil, reduce the heat to low and let it simmer uncovered, stirring continuously with a spatula. Cook until slightly reduced and thickened, 8 to 10 minutes. Remove and discard the cardamom pods. Stir in the pistachios and combine thoroughly.

2/ Pour the mixture into eight molds, dividing it evenly among them, and cover. Place the molds in the freezer until completely frozen, 4 to 6 hours. When ready to serve, gently invert the molds onto a platter. (If the kulfi don't come out easily, roll them in your hands for 5 to 10 seconds; the heat from your hands will help them release.) Serve immediately. (Alternatively, if you don't have molds, you can transfer the mixture to a freezer-safe container, cover, and freeze it for the same amount of time. When ready to serve, allow the kulfi to rest at room temperature for 2 to 3 minutes before serving individual scoops.)

Five-Ingredient Dulce de Leche Brownies

● **MAKES ONE 9-INCH ROUND BROWNIE**

Chances are, if you bought this book (thank you!), you know I love a good food hack. Sometimes you want something really easy, with just a few ingredients, that's still really delicious, and this recipe is for those times.

The brownie itself is made from just three ingredients: Oreos, eggs, and sour cream. Hack #1: I use cookies instead of a more complicated mixture of flour, cocoa, and sugar in the batter. Not only is this less time-consuming, but the texture is unbelievably fudgy, moist, and tender—while developing this recipe, I started calling it a "crownie," because it really tastes like a mix between a cake and a brownie. So decadent and delicious! You cook the dulce de leche topping *in* the can it comes in, so it couldn't be easier, but is as delicious as many more elaborate caramel variations. (Hack #2!) The only other thing you need is a little flaky sea salt to have a truly delicious five-ingredient dessert!

1 (14-ounce) can sweetened condensed milk

30 Oreos (from a 14.3-ounce package)

3 large eggs, separated

½ cup (120g) sour cream

Nonstick cooking spray

Flaky sea salt, for garnish

1/ Remove the label from the can of condensed milk. Place the can in a large saucepot and add water to cover by at least an inch. Bring to a boil over high heat, then reduce the heat to medium-low and simmer for 3 hours, rotating the can occasionally with tongs. Bring a small saucepot or kettle of water to a simmer to use as needed to top off the water in the large saucepot. (Never allow the water to drop below the top of the can.) After 3 hours, carefully remove the can from the water with tongs and let it cool for several hours to room temperature. (The dulce de leche will keep in the refrigerator for 2 to 3 weeks.)

2/ To bake the brownie, preheat the oven to 350°F.

3/ Combine the Oreos, egg yolks, and sour cream in the bowl of a food processor. Process until smooth. Transfer the mixture to a large bowl and set aside.

4/ In the bowl of a stand mixer fitted with the whisk attachment, beat the egg whites until stiff peaks form, 4 to 5 minutes. Fold one-third of the egg whites into the Oreo mixture to lighten it. Gently fold in the rest of the egg whites until just combined.

5/ Lightly grease a 9-inch springform pan with the nonstick cooking spray and pour in the Oreo mixture. Bake until the middle is just barely set, 20 to 25 minutes. Transfer the pan to a cooling rack until cool enough to handle, then release the clamp and remove the sides from the pan, and transfer the brownie onto a cooling rack. Pour the dulce de leche over the top and, using an offset spatula, spread it almost to the edge, leaving a ½-inch border. Garnish with flaky salt and slice it into individual wedges to serve.

QUICK BITE

If for some reason you can't make the dulce de leche on the stovetop, don't worry! It can be made in the oven: Preheat the oven to 425°F and pour the can of sweetened condensed milk into an 8 × 8-inch glass baking or pie dish, cover it with foil, and place it in a roasting pan. Fill the roasting pan with hot water to come halfway up the side of the dish and bake for 2 hours. Then follow the rest of the instructions in the main method for cooling and storing.

Cookies & Cream Ice Cream Pie

● **MAKES ONE 8-INCH ROUND PIE**

We've established in this chapter that I don't love cake, and so for every birthday as a kid, my parents got me an ice cream cake instead. I have yet another confession to make: I don't really love chocolate ice cream either, but I know almost everyone else does, and THAT is why this cookies and cream ice cream pie is a truly delicious compromise.

There's lots of rich, creamy vanilla ice cream for me in this dessert and chocolate cookie bits flecked throughout for the chocolate lovers. I love cookies in ice cream especially because the cookies don't get hard and lose their flavor the way chocolate chips do when they're frozen! And if the chocolate cookies aren't enough, there's a warm, rich, fudgy chocolate sauce in this recipe, too. This means you can have whatever chocolate-to-vanilla ratio you want, and everyone at the party is happy. What more could you ask from a pie?!

ICE CREAM PIE

- 30 Oreos (from a 14.3-ounce package)
- ½ stick (55g) unsalted butter, melted
- 1 quart cookies and cream ice cream, softened to a spreadable consistency

CHOCOLATE FUDGE SAUCE

- 4 ounces (113g) unsweetened chocolate, chopped
- 3 tablespoons (41g) unsalted butter, at room temperature
- ¾ cup (150g) sugar
- ⅔ cup (163g) whole milk
- 1 teaspoon cornstarch
- 1 teaspoon pure vanilla extract
- ½ teaspoon kosher salt

1/ Line the bottom and sides of an 8-inch springform pan with plastic wrap, leaving enough over the sides so that it will be able to wrap across the top as well. Prepare a space in your freezer large enough for the pan, making sure it can set flat and level.

2/ **MAKE THE PIE** In the bowl of a food processor, pulse the Oreos until fine crumbs form. Pour in the melted butter and pulse until combined and the mixture resembles wet sand.

3/ Dump the cookie crumbs out into the prepared springform pan and, using your hands or a flat-bottomed measuring cup, press them into an even layer. (If the cookies are sticky, spray your hands or the measuring cup with a little nonstick cooking spray.) Top with the softened ice cream, spreading it into an even layer. Cover tightly with the plastic wrap and set in the freezer for at least 6 hours, or until very firm.

4/ **MAKE THE CHOCOLATE FUDGE SAUCE** Just before serving, place the chocolate and butter in a small heavy-bottomed saucepan set over low heat. Cook until completely melted, then stir in the sugar, milk, and cornstarch and cook over low heat, stirring often, until the sauce begins to thicken and the sugar has dissolved. Remove from the heat and stir in the vanilla and salt.

5/ To serve, remove the pie from the springform pan. (The pie can be eaten directly out of the freezer, but if you want a softer ice cream, let it sit out for up to 30 minutes.) Carefully slice the pie into wedges and top each slice with a spoonful of the fudge sauce before serving. (Leftover pie can be wrapped tightly in plastic and kept in the freezer for up to 2 weeks. Leftover chocolate fudge sauce will keep in an airtight jar in the refrigerator for up to 1 week.)

Resources

When I was a kid and first got interested in cooking, I was OBSESSED with reading books, watching documentaries, and looking at every blog I could find to teach myself about food from around the world. Learning about different techniques and cuisines through books and shows is still one of my favorite things to do. Here are some of the sources that inspired me to learn more about food, gave me ideas for creating my own recipes, and helped give me confidence to get in the kitchen. I hope by sharing these, you will become as excited and interested in cooking as I did!

DOCUMENTARIES + TV SERIES

Chef's Table

Cooked, hosted by Michael Pollan

Ella Brennan: Commanding the Table, directed by Leslie Iwerks

Follow the Food

In Search of Israeli Cuisine, hosted by Michael Solomonov

Iron Chef

Jiro Dreams of Sushi, directed by David Gelb

Kings of Pastry

A Matter of Taste: Serving Up Paul Liebrandt, directed by Sally Rowe

Salt Fat Acid Heat, hosted by Samin Nosrat

BOOKS

Black Girl Baking: Wholesome Recipes Inspired by a Soulful Upbringing, by Jerrelle Guy

BraveTart: Iconic American Desserts, by Stella Parks

Casa Marcela: Recipes and Food Stories of My Life in the Californias, by Marcela Valladolid

Chaat: Recipes from the Kitchens, Markets, and Railways of India, by Maneet Chauhan and Jody Eddy

The Complete Book of Indian Cooking, by Shehzad Husain and Rafi Fernandez

The Complete Indian Regional Cookbook: 300 Classic Recipes from the Great Regions of India, by Mridula Baljekar

Curries Without Worries: An Introduction to Indian Cuisine, by Sudha Koul

50 Great Curries of India, by Camellia Panjabi

The Flavor Bible: The Essential Guide to Culinary Creativity, Based on the Wisdom of America's Most Imaginative Chefs, by Karen Page and Andrew Dornenburg

Indian-ish: Recipes and Antics from a Modern American Family, by Priya Krishna with Ritu Krishna

An Invitation to Indian Cookery, by Madhur Jaffrey

Joy the Baker Cookbook: 100 Simple and Comforting Recipes, by Joy Wilson

Jubilee: Recipes from Two Centuries of African American Cooking, by Toni Tipton-Martin

Larousse Gastronomique: The World's Greatest Culinary Encyclopedia, by Librairie Larousse

Maangchi's Big Book of Korean Cooking: From Everyday Meals to Celebration Cuisine, by Maangchi with Martha Rose Shulman

Madhur Jaffrey's World Vegetarian: More Than 650 Meatless Recipes from Around the World, by Madhur Jaffrey

Mexico: The Cookbook, by Margarita Carrillo Arronte

Molly on the Range: Recipes and Stories from an Unlikely Life on a Farm, by Molly Yeh

Notes from a Young Black Chef: A Memoir, by Kwame Onwuachi with Joshua David Stein

On Food and Cooking: The Science and Lore of the Kitchen, by Harold McGee

Ottolenghi Simple: A Cookbook, by Yotam Ottolenghi with Tara Wigley and Esme Howarth

Ramen Obsession: The Ultimate Bible for Mastering Japanese Ramen, by Naomi Imatome-Yun and Robin Donovan

Recipes from an Indian Kitchen: Authentic Recipes from Across India, by Sunil Vijayakar

Season: Big Flavors, Beautiful Food, by Nik Sharma

The Spice Cookbook, by Avanelle Day and Lillie Stuckey

Taco USA: How Mexican Food Conquered America, by Gustavo Arellano

Vegetable Kingdom: The Abundant World of Vegan Recipes, by Bryant Terry

Yes, Chef: A Memoir, by Marcus Samuelsson with Veronica Chambers

Zahav: A World of Israeli Cooking, by Michael Solomonov and Steven Cook

Zoe's Ghana Kitchen: An Introduction to New African Cuisine—from Ghana with Love, by Zoe Adjonyoh

CHEFS + COOKS

Guy Fieri

Hetty McKinnon

Julia Turshen

Marcus Samuelsson

Rick Martinez

Sohla El-Waylly

Tabitha Brown

Acknowledgments

Every time I've mentioned to a cookbook author that I wanted to write a cookbook of my own, they have all warned me how inconceivably massive, yet rewarding, the process is. As a mildly (some would say overly) confident teenager, I'd convinced myself that I'd defy all odds and put out this book entirely by myself. Based on the length of this acknowledgments page, you have probably already figured out that I was quite mistaken! Not only did this book take a village, but I also never anticipated how much joy the process of working on it with such talented individuals would bring. Though my name is on the cover, this book was truly a team effort and the result of the hard work of many.

First off, I have to thank the incredible team at Clarkson Potter and everyone under the larger Penguin Random House umbrella, particularly my editor, Jennifer Sit. Jenn: Thank you for believing in my vision for this book and using your expertise to refine it to the beautiful work of art it has become. I could not have asked for a better editor. Thank you, as well, Jen Wang, for translating my words into this gorgeous design; Kim Tyner and Joyce Wong in production and production editorial; Stephanie Davis in marketing; and Natalie Yera in publicity.

Thank you, Caitlin Leffel, for your painstaking work polishing this book and making sure my recipes and ideas are understandable in every kitchen.

To my managers, Stephanie Piza and Desiree Ansari, and the entire UNCMMN team: Thank you for being the best (and most FUN!) managers I could have ever asked for.

Thank you to my incredible team at WME: Lauren Zelner, Josh Upfal, Jenna Praeger, Sydney Kobil, Kate Lonczak, Chelsea Kreps, and most importantly for this book, my wonderful literary agent, Sabrina Taitz! Sabrina, your work ethic, expert guidance, unwavering enthusiasm, and support have made my dream for this book possible! Thank you for keeping me sane through every bump in the road, no matter the frequency or the hour of my endless FaceTime calls.

To my amazing team at Mona Creative, Eva, Lindsay, and Vanessa: Thank you for listening to all of my wild ideas for promoting this book and putting them into action. You all got my vision from the start and championed everything PR with unmatched expertise. You guys are a first-time author's dream team.

Thanks also to my amazing team at Made In Network, Ben, Emilija, Josh, Kevin, and Ross: I'm constantly in awe of your talent and creativity. You guys channeled my vision for YouTube to a level I could have never imagined.

To my legal team, namely Ashley Silver, thank you for crossing every *t* and dotting every *i*.

To my incredibly talented photography team, Mark Weinberg, Lauren LaPenna, Sophie Strangio, Scott Fletcher, Tiffany Schleigh, Nina Guevara, Patrice Clonts, and Kyle Acebo: I couldn't have picked a better group of people to shoot this book. You guys killed every photo, dish, and prop, and this book simply wouldn't be as beautiful as it is without each of you. Your collective creative mastery, experience, and energy on set were endlessly inspiring. Thank you for bringing your incredible talent (and incredible sense of humor) to set during some of the craziest two weeks of my life.

To ensure these recipes will work perfectly every time, not only in my kitchen but yours, too, a huge thank-you to Molly Adams and Sara Tane for testing every single recipe in this book. Your attention to detail and masterful feedback were so valuable to the recipe writing process.

To Rachel Dolfi, my incomparable executive culinary producer at Eitan Productions: As the first full-time person hired at Eitan Productions, you were an irreplaceable part of this book process. As the project manager of this book, you masterfully steered the ship of its creation process and kept me on track the entire time, and your vast culinary expertise was invaluable in refining the recipes that went in it. To say that I'm grateful for the time, energy, and knowledge you put into making this book is an understatement.

To Olivia Anderson, my multitalented senior culinary producer at Eitan Productions: From the moment we met on FaceTime, I knew we'd have a blast working together both in and out of the kitchen. Somehow within just a few months of meeting, you were able to help me put the words that I had in my head on paper in a way that to this day blows my mind. Your culinary knowledge and baking expertise were especially helpful in the testing process.

To Noah Schultz, my indescribably talented and caring friend and head of operations at Eitan Productions: Thank you for being the glue that holds the Eitan Productions team together. You've supported so many components of this journey, from late-night/last-minute grocery store runs for hard-to-find ingredients to managing the complex postproduction operations, all long before your role with the company was even formalized. You've been an endlessly gracious friend during one of the most exciting, albeit stressful, times of my life. Most important, thanks for making sure I always spent at least some part of each day being a normal teenager in between the craziness.

To Kristin Wiewel, my incredible personal assistant at Eitan Productions: I am so grateful for how quickly you became part of the EP team. Your enthusiasm, organization, and creativity are like no other. Thank you for championing all my crazy ideas and making sure everything going on in my life stays in one piece.

To Jin Ko, assistant video editor at Eitan Productions: Thank you for putting together promo videos, the behind-the-scenes story of the book, and all the other amazing content you edit on a daily basis.

To my friends Alyssa, Ari, Ben S., Ben T., Britney, Dara, Eliana, Goldie, Henya, Hibah, Jared, Josh, Lital, Manny, Natan, Rami, Sam D, Sam L, Ving, and more: Thank you for your love and support and being the fuel to my fire.

To Cardi Bernath, director of Paw-blicity at Eitan Productions: Thank you for making sure every dish in the book has a purr-fect balance of flavors. You are never shy to mark your territory, and really shaped this book over the last year (although you describe it as feeling like seven) with your sixth sense of the industry and ability to sniff out all the best flavors. Thank you for all you do.

To Ernie, director of Pup-Lick Relations at Eitan Productions: Though you joined the company with zero training (including potty), you have quickly excelled with your ability to build friendships, melt hearts, and mark your territory anywhere and everywhere you please. As a level K-9 chef, your feedback was invaluable to make sure we were paws-itive every recipe in this book was perfect.

To Yoni, my partner in crime and the one person who can always make me laugh: Thank you for being the funniest brother I could ever have asked for. You are always there for me through the good and bad and, of course, ALWAYS make sure I stay humble. ;)

To Grandma Linda and Grandma Bobbie: Thank you for being a constant and limitless source of love, comfort, and support. I feel wildly privileged to have both of you in my life and to have the close relationship and bond we share. I cherish my time with each of you, am grateful for every memory we've made together, and am honored to have been able to share a recipe from each of you in this book.

Most important of all, I want to thank my mom and dad for their unwavering support, endless love, and (of course) bringing me into the world on April 25, 2002. My success has only been possible because of the many sacrifices you've made my entire life to make it happen. Thank you for believing in my dreams long before anyone else did, no matter how unimaginable they were. When everyone told you that you were crazy for letting your kid compete on national television at age eleven, converting our garage into a film studio, allowing me to take over the home kitchen for cooking and filming around the clock, and the innumerable sacrifices and inconveniences (many that I probably never even knew about), you did so with genuine excitement and belief in the dream I was building. None of my success would have been possible without you not only allowing me to pursue my passion but encouraging, celebrating, and working with me every step of the way.

Index

ISBN 978-0-593-23536-2
Ebook ISBN 978-0-593-23537-9

Printed in China

Book and cover design by Jen Wang
Cover photographs by Mark Weinberg

Photographer: Mark Weinberg
Digital Tech: Kyle Acebo
Food Stylist: Lauren LaPenna
Food Stylist Assistants: Scott Fletcher and Tiffany Schleigh
Prop Stylist: Sophie Strangio
Prop Stylist Assistant: Nina Guevara
Groomer: Patrice Clonts
Executive Culinary Producer: Rachel Dolfi
Senior Culinary Producer: Olivia Anderson
Director of Operations: Noah Schultz

Editor: Jennifer Sit
Editorial Assistant: Bianca Cruz
Designer: Jen Wang
Production Editor: Joyce Wong
Production Manager: Kim Tyner
Compositors: Zoe Tokushige and Hannah Hunt
Copy Editor: Kathy Brock
Indexer: Elizabeth Parson
Marketer: Stephanie Davis
Publicist: Natalie Yera

10 9 8 7 6 5 4 3 2 1

First Edition